THE WISDOM AND HEALING POWER OF WHOLE FOODS

The ultimate handbook for using foods and lifestyle changes to bolster your body's ability to repair and regulate itself.

by Patrick Quillin, PhD,RD,CNS

Nutrition Times Press, Inc.

Other books by Patrick Quillin (website: www.PatrickQuillin.com)
-BEATING CANCER WITH NUTRITION, Nutrition Times Press, Carlsbad, CA, 2005
-ADJUVANT NUTRITION IN CANCER TREATMENT, Cancer Treatment Research
Foundation, Arlington Heights, IL, 1994
-HEALING NUTRIENTS, Contemporary Books, Chicago, 1987

Available exclusively from:
NTP,Inc., Box 130789, Carlsbad, CA 92013, ph.760-804-5703
website: www.GettingHealthier.com

TELL US YOUR STORY
We want to hear your experiences about using this book as part of your healthy
lifestyle. Please send us your personal experience (email: pq@patrickquillin.com)
with an address or phone number on how to contact you. Your story may provide
hope and inspiration for others suffering from the same condition. Thank you.

DEDICATION
My utmost admiration and appreciation go forth to the bold
physicians, scientists and healers throughout history who were more
concerned with their patient's welfare than peer approval.

IMPORTANT NOTICE!!! PLEASE READ!!!
The information in this book is meant to be used in conjunction with the
guidance of your health care professional. The information presented
here is neither advice nor prescriptions, but provided for educational
purposes only. If you think you have a medical problem, then please
seek qualified professional help immediately. In the event that you use
this information without your doctor's approval, you are prescribing for
yourself, which is your constitutional right, but the publisher and author
assume no responsibility. If you cannot accept these conditions, then
you may return this book in new condition for a full refund. Do not use
this information as sole therapy against any disease. Nutrition
supplements and food products described in this book are not intended
to diagnose, treat, cure or prevent any disease. This information has not
been evaluated by the Food and Drug Administration.

CONTENTS

EXECUTIVE SUMMARY

"Natural forces within us are the true healers." Hippocrates, father of modern medicine, circa 400 BC

♥ If you are too tired to read this entire book, then please read this short summary to get you started.

♥ There are simple solutions to be found in nature. When we learn our nutrition from nature, we find that whole foods contain an elegant symphony of nutrients that go beyond our basic nutrition textbooks. Eating whole foods nourishes the body so that it can regulate and repair itself.

♥ Americans eat foods that have been stripped of nutrient content. The most commonly eaten vegetables in America are catsup, French fries and onion rings, which are not whole foods and have been heavily processed. Our epidemic proportions of cancer, heart disease, diabetes, obesity, Alzheimer's, and more are often created by our highly refined diet.

♥ American health care is nearing a meltdown point. We have, by far, the world's most expensive health care system, costing us $2.2 trillion per year, or 16% of the gross domestic product, which is bankrupting huge corporations, like General Motors, and threatens to bankrupt our nation. We cannot buy good health while continuing to ignore the basic laws of nature: "you are what you eat", and "our way of life is related to our way of death".

♥ Weight loss is a major imperative in America. Over two thirds of Americans are overweight, while half of these people are medically obese. It is easy to lose weight on a diet rich in fruits and vegetables, which are primarily fiber and water. It is difficult to lose weight on the standard diet high in calorie dense foods.

♥ Diabetes has become a huge problem in American health care. Eating too much and the wrong foods is a major contributor to our diabetes epidemic.

♥ Cancer has escalated from an obscure disease in 1900 to the number one cause of death in 2005. There are abundant studies showing that a diet rich in whole fruits and vegetables can dramatically lower the risk for cancer.

CHAPTER 1
LEARNING NUTRITION
FROM NATURE

"Look deep into nature, and then you will understand everything better."Albert Einstein, Nobel prize winner in physics 1921, founder of the nuclear age

FROM NATURE'S PHARMACY: DIM from cruciferous vegetables. In the 1950s, researchers gave two different types of diets to rats, then exposed them to radioactivity, as if they were near a nuclear blast. The rats who ate beets had a higher incidence of cancer than the rats who ate broccoli, so the researchers concluded that something in beets makes radioactivity more toxic. Two decades later, Lee Wattenberg, MD of the University of Minnesota discovered the truth regarding this previous study: there are compounds in broccoli that reduce the toxicity of radioactivity and other cancer-causing agents. The enlightened era of chemo-prevention was born. Scientists have

isolated various indoles in cruciferous vegetables (broccoli, Brussels sprout, cabbage, kale, cauliflower, etc.). DIM (diindolylmethane) is one of the more promising phytonutrients that may help to reduce the damaging effects of toxins, including excess estrogens in the body. Although DIM and indoles are not considered essential nutrients, yet, they are quite valuable if you are interested in lowering your cancer risk and improving general health.

There is a mysterious yet irreplaceable force in all of life that "knows" how to heal itself. The broken bone, the scab on your arm, the baby being made in that woman's uterus, the ability of children to regenerate a severed fingertip--all tell us that Nature has an incredible plan for good health and long life. But only if those same natural forces within us have been given the raw building blocks of physical nutrients and metaphysical thoughts and feelings, plus relative freedom from toxic blockages.

WHAT IS NOT IN WHOLE FOODS?

antibiotics
growth hormones
pesticides
herbicides
fungicides
hormone disrupters
toxic metals (i.e. arsenic)
aflatoxins (fungal by products)
etc.

WHAT IS IN WHOLE FOODS?

Nature to be commanded must be obeyed.
Sir Francis Bacon (1561-1626) founder of scientific inquiry

"Look deep into nature and then you will understand everything better." Albert Einstein

Without food processing we wouldn't know much about human nutrition. That's right. When European sailors spent months at sea with an imbalanced diet lacking in fresh fruits and vegetables, they came down with scurvy. Half of all trans-oceanic explorers from 1600-1850 died from this common vitamin C deficiency. When we taught the Indonesians how to refine whole rice down to white rice, thus removing the valuable thiamin, we began the beri-beri (literally means "I cannot, I cannot") disease of thiamin deficiency. When we decided to remove the fiber from whole fruits, vegetables and grains, we began history's greatest epidemic outbreaks of obesity, heart disease, cancer and more. When we naively thought that we could duplicate the nutritional value of mother's milk for newborn infants, we later learned of all the minute but critical components in mother's milk. Every time we think that we can improve on nature, we find our confidence misplaced. Every time we fiddle with a wholesome food, we erode its nutrient value. This message is the take home lesson from this book: In whole foods lies a universe of nutrients that we will never fully understand but are there for our benefit. Extracting juice from fruits and vegetables makes as much sense as eating white flour.

JUICING VERSUS PUREEING. Some of the earlier efforts

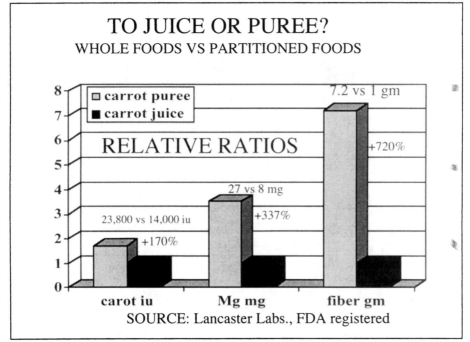

TO JUICE OR PUREE?
WHOLE FOODS VS PARTITIONED FOODS

□ carrot puree
■ carrot juice

RELATIVE RATIOS

7.2 vs 1 gm
+720%

27 vs 8 mg
+337%

23,800 vs 14,000 iu
+170%

carot iu   Mg mg   fiber gm

SOURCE: Lancaster Labs., FDA registered

at relieving illness with nutrition involved diets high in vegetables with regular fruit and vegetable juices offered throughout the day. Juicing has its advantages, because one glass of carrot juice is equal to about a pound of carrots, which few of us could eat. Unfortunately, much of the valuable anti-cancer nutrients in the vegetables get tossed out with the pulp that is discarded. Better yet, use a high speed blender, such as my choice, Vitamix (Vitamix.com), which will keep all the valuable nutrients in while allowing you to consume more vegetables in a liquid form. There are 10 times more health giving phytochemical agents in pureed whole vegetables than in juice extracted from vegetable pulp.

Can a healthy lifestyle lower overall mortality?

Hale Project: 1507 healthy men + 832 women, ages 70-90, 11 countries Europe, 12 year followup (1988-2000), adherence to Mediterranean diet, exercise, no smoking, moderate alcohol

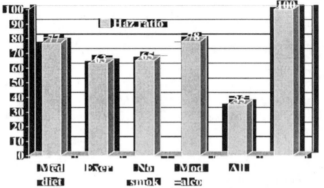

Conclusions: "adherence to a Mediterranean diet and healthful lifestyle is associated with a more than 50% lower rate of all-causes mortality." (95%CI) *Knoops, KT, JAMA, 2004;292:1433-9*

DOES DIET REALLY MATTER IN HEALTH? How rich could a drug company get if they offered a patented medication that could lower all cause mortality by 50%? That is what a healthy lifestyle can do! Researchers followed 2300 men and women in 11 countries in Europe over the course of 12 years. The people were monitored for their diet, smoking, exercise, and alcohol intake. Exercise cut risk of all cause mortality by 37%, not smoking by 35%, moderate alcohol intake by 22% and Mediterranean diet (whole grains, legumes, fresh fruit, vegetables, low in animal food) by 23%. When combined, this healthy lifestyle cut all cause mortality by more than 50%.

Food is a rich tapestry of thousands of substances, including ingredients that we are only beginning to understand. Food provides the macronutrients that direct the extremely influential hormones and prostaglandins in your body. Food contains known essential vitamins, minerals, and "sub-nutrients" along with some very intriguing conditionally essential nutrients (like lycopenes and ellagic acid) that can bring us beyond surviving a life of chronic illness into thriving with optimal health and vitality.

CAN LIFESTYLE IMPROVE THE REPAIR OF DEFECTIVE DNA (CANCER)?

Study design: 30 men with indolent prostate cancer (PSA 4.8) were assessed for gene expression profiles from prostate cancer needle biopsy at DX and 3 months after beginning intervention lifestyle program.

Results: Micro arrays detected 48 up regulated and 453 down regulated transcripts after intervention. Side benefits included: inc.mental health, dec. BMI, BP, LDL, chol*, triglyc, CRP, waist line (8 cm)

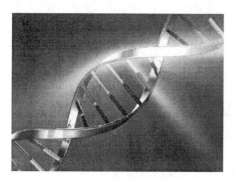

Intervention:
Diet (plant based, whole food, low fat 11% kcal)
Exercise (3.6 hr/wk)
Stress management (4.5 hr/wk)

CONCLUSIONS: This pilot study is the first to show genetic changes in cancer patients based solely on lifestyle intervention.
Ornish, et al., PNAS, 105, 24, June 17, 2008

Our eating habits are all acquired. We base our current diet on what mother cooked when we were younger; what our society, ethnic and religious groups prefer; what is advertised in print and electronic media, and what is available in the local grocery store. People in the Philippines or the Amazon are born with structurally identical taste buds to Americans, yet they eat entirely different foods. Realize that it takes about 3 weeks to acquire new eating habits. Try this program for 3 weeks, at which time it will become easier to stay with and you may just find that the nutrient-depleted junk food of yesterday really doesn't satisfy your taste buds like the following whole foods.

SYNERGISTIC FORCES IN WHOLE FOODS

Although 1000 mg daily of vitamin C has been shown to reduce the risk for stomach cancer, a small glass of orange juice containing only 37 mg of vitamin C is twice as likely to lower the chances for stomach cancer. Something in whole oranges is even more chemo-protective than vitamin C. Although most people only absorb 20-50% of their ingested calcium, the remaining calcium binds up potentially damaging fats in the intestines to provide protection against colon cancer.

In 1963, a major "player" in the American drug business, Merck, tried to patent a single antibiotic substance that was originally isolated from yogurt. But this substance did not work alone. Since then, researchers have found no less than 7 natural antibiotics that all contribute to yogurt's unique ability to protect the body from infections. There are many anti-cancer agents in plant food, including over 800 mixed carotenoids, over 20,000 various bioflavonoids, lutein, lycopenes and canthaxanthin. The point is: we can isolate and concentrate certain factors in foods for use as therapeutic supplements in cancer therapy, but we must always rely heavily on the mysterious and elegant symphony of ingredients found in whole food.

ORAC: OXYGEN RADICAL ABSORBENCE CAPACITY
sponges for free radicals

ORAC/5 GM	
prunes 288	"...reduce risk of diseases of aging by adding high ORAC foods to diet." Floyd Horn, PhD, Tufts Univ.
raisins 141	
blueberries 111	
blackberries 101	
garlic 96	*need 3000-5000 ORAC units/day (food & supplements) average US intake 1200 ORAC*
kale 88	
cranberries 87	
strawberries 76	
spinach raw 60	
plum 47	

DIETARY RECOMMENDATIONS

Since the 1964 World Health Organization published their first pamphlet on cancer causes, many prominent health organizations have publicized their own personal version of a "healthy diet". Guidelines on good eating principles have come from the Senate Diet Goals, American Cancer Society, American Dietetic Association, Surgeon General of the United States, United States Public Health Association,

American Heart Association, and many more. While these programs have minor variations, they have much in common. Each of these programs embraces a diet that:

     -uses only unprocessed foods, nothing in a package with a label

     -uses high amounts of fresh vegetables

     -employs a low fat diet

     -emphasizes the importance of regularity

     -uses low fat dairy or no dairy products, with yogurt as the preferred dairy selection

     -stabilizes blood sugar levels with no sweets and never eat something sweet by itself

     -increases potassium and reduces sodium intake

NUTRIENT INTAKE IS CRUCIAL FOR ALL PLANTS AND ANIMALS ON EARTH
but not for humans?

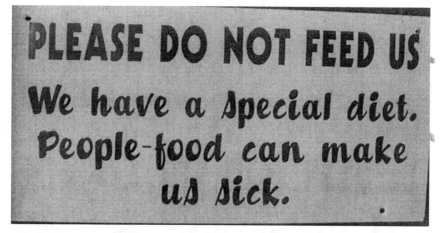

Talk to any farmer, animal lover, horse breeder, gardener, marine biologists, and such and you find the same common ground: what you feed the plants and animals will have a huge impact on the health of the plants and animals. Then we take Americans, most of whom are living on a diet of cadaverous empty calorie junk food, and use drugs to try to resolve health problems rather than using nutrition as front line therapy.

Go to a big city zoo or even a county fair where there are many animals in close contact with the general public and you will see a sign similar to the above warning: "People food can make us sick." And you have to wonder what food might kill a 400 pound ape that is acceptable or good for a 40 pound child.

We need to get back to the basics regarding health. What you put in your mouth becomes a powerful biological response modifier, changing the way the body works. This book offers insight on some of the basic tenets of healing: you are what you eat.

REASONS FOR OMNIVOROUS DIET

CARNIVORE NUTRIENTS	HERBIVORE nutrients
conjugated linoleic acid (CLA)	carotenoids
eicosapentaenoic acid (EPA)	bioflavonoids
cartilage (glycosaminoglycans)	sterolins (beta sitosterol)
carnitine	fiber (butyrate)
CoQ	potassium
B-12	anti-fungals (veg., mushr.,kelp)
zinc	chlorophyll
quarternary amino acid sequence	
biological value of protein	

IT IS NOT NICE TO FOOL WITH MOTHER NATURE

In the dark days of World War II, America was running short of foods. With the farmers drafted into the service and much food being shipped to the troops overseas, the government decided to support food rationing. Hydrogenated vegetable "oleo margarine" was offered as the acceptable substitute for butter. Take corn or safflower oil and expose it to a catalyst to "saturate" the carbon bonds with hydrogens. You end up with a fat that has similar taste and appearance to saturated fats in nature. Although on paper this substitution looked good, we have since found numerous reasons to ban or seriously discourage these unnatural fats. Trans fats can increase the risk for heart disease and many other health problems. "It is not nice to fool with mother nature." was a witty ad slogan of the 1970s.

There have been many experiments in trying to improve on nature. Most have been dramatic failures. Over 200 studies have shown that a diet rich in colorful fruits and vegetables lowers the risk for most cancers and heart disease. In nature, the native cis beta carotene is mixed with hundreds of other carotenoids and bioflavonoids in plant food. From this data, researchers decided to use all trans synthetic beta carotenoid which was then coated with coal tar derived food coloring for a scientific study in heavy smokers. Turns out the mono nutrient study using an unnatural vitamin increased the risk of lung cancer in heavy smokers. No surprise there.

Vitamin E was called the "vitamin in search of a disease" in the 1960s after a study deprived students ("volunteers") of vitamin E for a year and found no blatant deficiency symptoms. Turns out it takes longer for the symptoms of premature hemolysis (bursting of red blood cells) to surface in vitamin E deficiency. One study found that nurses taking 200 mg per day of vitamin E supplements lowered their risk for heart disease by 40%. Then came the chemical "tinkerers". Let's take nature's design for vitamin E, which is a rich mixture of tocopherols (alpha, beta, delta, gamma) plus tocotrienols (alpha, beta, delta, gamma) and instead create a synthetic vitamin E (synthetic d, l alpha tocopheryl acetate). No wonder the scientific studies using vitamin E have had mixed results.

Cows live on a diet of grass. They are ruminants, just like sheep, buffalo, and deer, with a multi-chambered stomach that allows them to convert the indigestible fiber from grass into usable sugar in the body. Agribusiness decided that cows do not grow fast enough (read: more profit) on a natural diet of grass. So the cows were put in massive feed lots, heads locked in feeders to prevent any movement (which would be a waste of calories), fed huge amounts of higher caloric density grains, given antibiotics to subdue the inevitable diseases that arise from crowded conditions while also stimulating growth by 20%, given multiple veterinarian drugs to combat the illnesses of living in unhygienic and cramped quarters, then fed the ground up parts of other cattle (a cow is a vegetarian and cannot digest animal products)...then we wonder why some studies have shown that beef can increase the risk for heart disease and cancer.

Yet, the Native Americans who ruled the central plains for centuries and followed the buffalo herds were very strong, athletic, and healthy people. They lived almost entirely on buffalo. Turns out that ruminants fed green grass generate a unique fatty acid, conjugated linoleic acid (CLA), that can lower the risk for cancer, heart disease, obesity, and many other conditions. Grass fed ruminants have 5 times more CLA than grain fed ruminants. Again, it is not nice to fool with mother nature. A lesson that we humans will eventually learn.

PATIENT PROFILE: R.T. was only 5 years old when he started developing attention deficit disorder. His teachers recommended prescription drugs. I suggested omega 3 oils to nourish his brain instead. While fish oil is best, flax oil is an acceptable omega 3 oil source. R.T.'s parents made a whole fruit smoothie with flax oil daily for R.T. Within 2 weeks, the parents called me at their astonishment in R.T.'s improved behavior. He was a bright kid who did not need medication. He needed essential fats for his brain to work properly.

CHAPTER 2
MALNUTRITION IN AMERICA
THE GREAT NUTRITION ROBBERY

"The doctor of the future will give no medicine, but will involve the patient in the proper use of food, fresh air and exercise." Thomas Edison

---

FROM NATURE'S PHARMACY: resveratrol

In spite of a high fat diet, the French have had a relatively low incidence of heart disease. Labeled the "French paradox", there is compelling evidence that resveratrol, found in red wine and other foods, may lower the risk for heart disease, cancer, diabetes, Alzheimer's and even slow the aging process. Resveratrol is found in the skin of red grapes and is produced by a few plants as a defense against attacking bacteria or fungi. All trans resveratrol (as compared to all cis-resveratrol) is the preferred and more active form of this substance. Some research finds that resveratrol may actually affect the genes (Sirtuin 1) that slow the aging process, just like calorie restriction. Resveratrol has demonstrated some activity at regulating blood glucose, preventing or slowing cancer growth, improving exercise capacity, and preventing the formation of plaques in the brain that cause Alzheimer's disease. Resveratrol is a polyphenol, which is an important class of phytochemicals. Other foods that are rich in polyphenols that have demonstrated health benefits include green tea, dark chocolate, pomegranates, apples and berries. Use 100% frozen grape juice concentrate as a liquid base for pureed whole fruit and veggie drinks. Delicious and good for you.

It is hard to believe that there can be malnutrition in this agriculturally abundant nation of ours--but there is. "Poor food choices" summarizes our dilemma at the dinner table. America is blessed to have enough food, but we are eating the wrong food and too much of it.

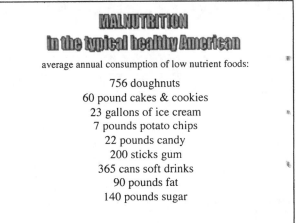

MALNUTRITION
in the typical healthy American

average annual consumption of low nutrient foods:

756 doughnuts
60 pound cakes & cookies
23 gallons of ice cream
7 pounds potato chips
22 pounds candy
200 sticks gum
365 cans soft drinks
90 pounds fat
140 pounds sugar

At the time of the Revolutionary War, 96% of Americans farmed while only 4% worked at other trades. Tractors and harvesting combines became part of an agricultural revolution that allowed the 2% of Americans who now farm to feed the rest of us. We grow enough food in this country (quantity) to feed ourselves, to make half of us overweight, to throw away enough food to feed 50 million people daily, to ship food overseas as a major export, and to store enough food in government surplus bins to feed Americans for a year if all farmers quit today. With so much food available, how can Americans be malnourished?

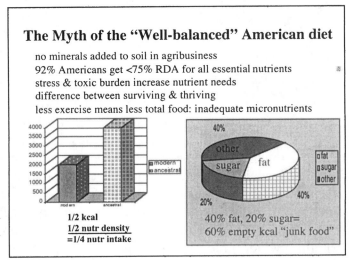

The Myth of the "Well-balanced" American diet

no minerals added to soil in agribusiness
92% Americans get <75% RDA for all essential nutrients
stress & toxic burden increase nutrient needs
difference between surviving & thriving
less exercise means less total food: inadequate micronutrients

1/2 kcal
1/2 nutr density
=1/4 nutr intake

40% fat, 20% sugar=
60% empty kcal "junk food"

MOST POPULAR GROCERY ITEMS IN AMERICA

1. Marlboro cigarettes
2. Coke Classic
3. Pepsi Cola
4. Kraft processed cheese
5. Diet Coke
6. Campbell's soup
7. Budweiser beer
8. Tide detergent
9. Folger's coffee
10. Winston cigarettes

from "1992 Top Ten Almanac" by Michael Robbins

TOP 3 VEGGIES IN AMERICA: CATSUP, FRENCH FRIES, ONION RINGS

The answer is: poor food choices. Americans choose their food based upon taste, cost, convenience, and psychological gratification--thus ignoring the main reason that we eat, which is to provide our body cells with the raw materials to grow, repair, and fuel our bodies. The most commonly eaten foods in America are white bread, coffee, and hot dogs. Based upon our food abundance, Americans could be the best nourished nation on record. But we are far from it.

CAUSES OF NUTRIENT DEFICIENCIES:

There are many reasons for developing malnutrition:

⇒ We don't eat well due to poor food choices, loss of appetite, discomfort in the gastrointestinal region, or consuming nutritionally bankrupt "junk food"; many people just don't get enough nutrients into their stomachs.

⇒ We don't absorb nutrients due to loss of digestive functions (including low hydrochloric acid or enzyme output), allergy, "leaky gut", or intestinal infections, like yeast overgrowth.

⇒ We don't keep enough nutrients due to increased excretion or loss of nutrients because of diarrhea, vomiting, or drug interactions.

⇒ We don't get enough nutrients due to increased requirements caused by fever, disease, alcohol, or drug interactions.

Anyone who is confused about why we spend so much on medical care with such poor results in cancer treatment might glean some wisdom by reading what sells best in American grocery stores. Overwhelming evidence from both government and independent scientific surveys shows that many Americans are low in their intake of a wide variety of nutrients:[1]

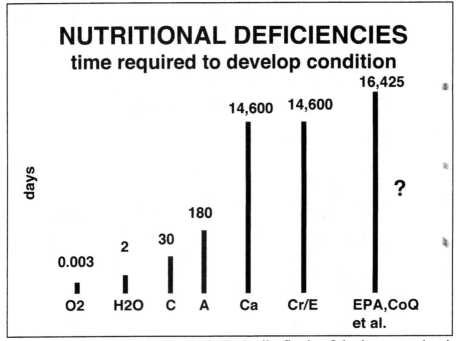

-VITAMINS: A, D, E, C, B-6, riboflavin, folacin, pantothenic acid

-MINERALS: calcium, potassium, magnesium, zinc, iron, chromium, selenium; and possibly molybdenum and vanadium. With many common micronutrient deficiencies in the Western diet, it makes sense that a major study in Australia found that regular use of vitamin supplements was a protective factor against colon cancer.[2]

-MACRONUTRIENTS: fiber, complex carbohydrates, plant protein, special fatty acids (EPA, GLA, ALA), clean water

Meanwhile, we also eat alarmingly high amounts of: fat, salt, sugar, cholesterol, alcohol, caffeine, food additives, and toxins.

This combination of too much of the wrong things along with not enough of the right things has created epidemic proportions of degenerative diseases in this country. The Surgeon General, Department of Health and Human Services, Center for Disease Control, National Academy of Sciences, American Medical Association, American Dietetic Association, and others agree that diet is a major contributor to our most common health problems.

The typical diet of the cancer patient is high in fat, while being low in fiber and vegetables--"meat, potatoes, and gravy" is what many of my patients lived on. Data collected by the United States

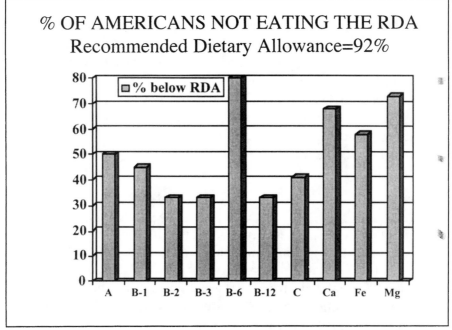

% OF AMERICANS NOT EATING THE RDA
Recommended Dietary Allowance=92%

Department of Agriculture from over 11,000 Americans showed that on any given day:

-41% did not eat any fruit

-82% did not eat cruciferous vegetables

-72% did not eat vitamin C-rich fruits or vegetables

-80% did not eat vitamin A-rich fruits or vegetables

-84% did not eat high fiber grain food, like bread or cereal[3]

The human body is incredibly resilient, which sometimes works to our disadvantage. No one dies on the first cigarette inhaled, or the first drunken evening, or the first decade of unhealthy eating. We misconstrue the fact that we survived this ordeal to mean we can do it forever. Not so. Malnutrition can be as blatant as the starving babies in third world countries, but malnutrition can also be much more subtle.

SEQUENCE IN DEVELOPING NUTRIENT DEFICIENCY

⇒ 1) *Preliminary.* Reduction of tissue stores and depression of urinary excretion.

⇒ 2) *Biochemical.* Reduction of enzyme activity due to insufficient coenzymes (vitamins). Urinary excretion at minimum levels.

⇒ 3) *Physiological.* Behavioral effects, such as insomnia or somnolence. Irritability accompanied by loss of appetite and reduced body weight. Modified drug metabolism and reduced immune capabilities.

⇒ 4) *Clinical.* Classical deficiency syndromes as recognized by the scientific pioneers in the developmental phases of nutrition science.

⇒ 5) *Terminal.* Severe tissue pathology resulting in imminent death.

PATIENT PROFILE: T.S. arrived on our hospital doorstep as a "medical emergency" in an ambulance. At age 53, he had been treated at a previous hospital for stage 4 lymphoma and failed therapy. Our team quickly realized that T.S. was dying from both cancer and malnutrition. Since he could not eat, we provided TPN (total parenteral nutrition) through his subclavian vein for a month, then got him on a good diet, then he was capable of tolerating our fractionated chemotherapy. Within 6 months, he was in complete remission. I saw him 7 years later and he was looking fabulous.

ENDNOTES

[1]. Quillin, P., HEALING NUTRIENTS, p.43, Vintage Books, NY, 1989
[2]. Kune, GA, and Kune, S., Nutrition and Cancer, vol.9, p.1, 1987
[3]. Patterson, BH, and Block, G., American Journal of Public Health, vol.78, p.282, Mar.1988

CHAPTER 3
HEALTH CARE MELTDOWN
THE SOLUTIONS TO OUR MULTI-TRILLION DOLLAR HEALTH CARE DEBACLE CAN BE FOUND IN NATURE

"Experts agree that our health care system is riddled with inefficiencies, excessive administrative expenses, inflated prices, poor management, and inappropriate care, waste and fraud."
National Coalition on Health Care, nchc.org 2009

FROM NATURE'S PHARMACY: IP6 and protease inhibitors. Did nature make a mistake? Whole grains and legumes contain a substance called phytic acid, which binds up minerals, especially iron, and escorts them out of the system. Phytic acid is a seed's way of storing phosphorus, like a school lunch bucket. For decades in the later 20th century, nutritionists thought that phytic acid must have been some mistake or "anti-nutrient" in whole grains and legumes, hence providing even more enthusiasm for processing grains down to white flour. In fact, we now find that phytic acid is one of the key ingredients in plant food lowering the risk for various cancers, kidney stones, heart disease, and liver disease. Best sources include beans, brown rice, sesame seeds, and corn. Phytic acid is now sold as a nutrition supplement: IP6, inositol hexaphosphate 6. In a similar vein, protease inhibitors are substances in legumes, especially soybeans, which can inhibit enzymes that break down protein in the gut. Again, nutritionists thought of protease inhibitors as "anti-nutrients". Raw legumes are unhealthy. However, there is now compelling evidence that these protease inhibitors actually are very therapeutic in retarding cancer growth, and even allowing humans to better tolerate radiation without serious side effects. Protease inhibitor drugs are now the fashionable trend in the pharmaceutical industry in slowing down the growth of viruses, including AIDS. Nature knows what it is doing. Do not bet against the wisdom of whole foods.

HEALTH CARE CREATED BY DR. FRANKENSTEIN

The cost of health care in America is obscene. Only the super rich and indigent are covered by adequate health insurance. For the 47 million Americans with no health insurance, health catastrophes have become a primary reason for bankruptcy and divorce. If you are on Welfare, Social Security, or other government doles, then you have some security against health problems. Border states from California to Florida spend many billions annually treating illegal aliens and providing full neonatal care for their newborns, who then become "anchor" babies, allowing the parents to become legal citizens. Yet millions of tax paying American-born citizens have no health care.

HEALTH STATE OF THE UNION

US #1 WORLD HEALTH EXPENSES $2 trillion/year
US #37 HEALTH CARE SYSTEM, according to World Health Org.
HEART DISEASE: 50% of deaths, more ER, RX, disability
CANCER: #1 cause death in US; from 3% of deaths in 1900 to 24% in 1999; 42% of Americans will develop cancer in lifetime, 8 mil treated, another 7 mil "in remission", 250%^ br.ca. 1950
DIABETES: 20 million inUS, 120 mil around world
MIND DRUGS: 131 mil RX psychoactive 1988 to 233 mil 1998
MEDICATION: 3rd-5th cause death US; 140,000/yr, 9.6 mil rxn/yr
OBESITY: 60% US, 300% ^ morbid OB since 1980, 90% type 2 DB
ASPIRIN: 55 billion per year in US
ALZHEIMER'S: 4 mil US, 14 mil 2050, 4th leading cause death US
HYPERTENSION: 60 million in US, RX increases risk for heart att.
INFECTIONS: from obscure to 3rd cause death, drug resistant strains

---

And if you really want full medical, dental, and psychiatric coverage for free, then commit a crime. I am not kidding. In 1976, the U.S. Supreme Court ruled that prisoners are entitled to full medical, dental, vision, psychiatric, and pharmaceutical benefits. California is on the ragged edge of bankruptcy and thus must release 55,000 prisoners because their prison care is considered inadequate. In March of 2009, a court appointed receiver ordered the state of California to spend $8 billion to upgrade prison medical facilities in spite of the $42 billion deficit the state faces.

HEALTH CARE COSTS:
public and private, as % GDP

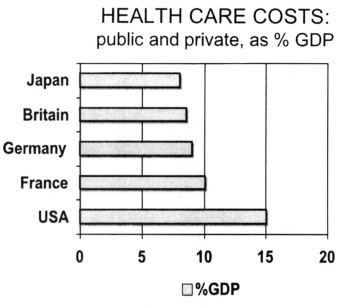

source: Economist, May 30, 2009, p.12

America spent $2.4 trillion in 2007 on disease maintenance, which was 17% of our gross national product--twice the expense per capita of any other health care system on earth. Notice that I said "disease maintenance", because we certainly do not support health care in America, and "health insurance" is neither related to health nor solid actuarial insurance. Health care for the indigent is the primary expense in many state budgets. The United States spends 6 times more per capita on the administration of our health care system than its peer Western European nations.

    A SILVER LINING? Before we dive into the gloomy statistics on the American health care system, let's touch on the good news. Life expectancy for Americans has increased from 50 years in 1900 to 78 years in 2009. Microsurgery on eyes (Lasik) and joints (arthroscopic) would have dazzled the famous futurist, Jules Verne. Pain management and emergency medical procedures can allow catastrophic injuries a chance at healing. Yet, in spite of the exotic arsenal of drugs, diagnostic tools, and procedures available to modern medicine, the most significant improvement in the health of modern humans, according to the first heart transplant surgeon, Christiaan Barnard, MD, was the invention of the indoor flushing toilet in

England in the 18th century, thus ending many plagues from fecal contamination.

Like the auto industry in Detroit, our American health care system is in dire need of reform. All the more reason to take care of your health and that of your family. Prevention is a key to avoiding this health care nightmare that reigns in America. And eating whole foods is an irreplaceable link in your wellness program. You need to take charge of your own health, because the government or your health insurance provider (if you have one) may not be able to do so.

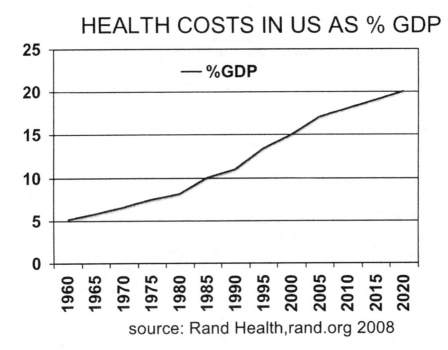

HEALTH COSTS IN US AS % GDP

source: Rand Health,rand.org 2008

NATION OF DRUG ADDICTS

No one with a headache is suffering from a deficiency of aspirin. No one with elevated cholesterol has a deficiency of statin drugs. No one with depression has a deficiency of Prozac. While drugs can provide short term valuable relief in health problems, drugs are usually not recommended for long term care, which is what happens in millions of Americans.

Nancy Reagan offered a catchy phrase during her term as the first lady of the White House "just say no to drugs". To be sure,

America has a problem with illicit drugs. But we have an equal or greater problem with prescription drugs. They are overused, expensive, dangerous, and often unnecessary. While America comprises 5% of the world's population, we consume 40% of the world's prescription medication. Every winter, nearly one million "snow bird" seniors gather along the Mexican border in their RVs in California and Arizona to have access to cheaper (by 30-50%) but identical prescription drugs found in Mexico. A professor at Harvard Medical School, John Abramson, MD, has written a brilliant and well documented book, OVERDOSED AMERICA, showing that lifestyle changes (diet, exercise, stop smoking, stress reduction) can offer cheaper, safer, and more effective healing from illness than prescription drugs.

Of the worldwide $600 billion pharmaceutical industry, $250 billion is in the United States. Drug companies underwrite 90% of continuing medication education, giving them inordinate control over physician awareness of drug strengths and limitations. Although Americans were issued 3.4 billion prescriptions in 2003 (12 per man, woman, and child) we rank 29th in life expectancy in the world.

Maybe the costs of these drugs would be more acceptable if they actually cured or relieved more symptoms than they created. In the past 6 years over 65,000 lawsuits have been filed against American drug makers. According to an article in the Journal of the American Medical Association, the proper use of prescription drugs is the 4th leading cause of death in America, killing somewhere between 100,000 and 140,000 Americans annually.[1] According to a review of the literature by a physician and naturopath, Carolyn Dean, MD, ND, in her book, DEATH BY MODERN MEDICINE, more like 780,000 Americans die each year from modern medicine.

Prescription drugs are approved based upon clinical trials published in peer reviewed scientific literature. Now we find out that many of these researchers are fabricating data or "bending" the study to suit the needs of the drug manufacturer. The former Editor in Chief, Marcia Angell, MD, of the blue chip medical journal the New England Journal of Medicine, has written a scathing expose, THE TRUTH ABOUT THE DRUG COMPANIES, stating that many medical reports are nothing more than unvarnished marketing reports from the drug manufacturers.

Then we start discussing the decadent markup on prescription drugs. While discount stores, like WalMart, might typically markup an item by 10%, and vitamins typically have a 200-400% markup. Markup from drugs goes up to 569,000%, or 5,690 times cost.

WHAT PRESCRIPTION DRUGS REALLY COST				
BRAND NAME®	DOSAGE	PRICE $/ 100 CAPS	COST $ GENERIC ACTIVE INGREDIENT	PERCENT MARKUP
Celebrex	100 mg	$130.27	$0.60	21,612%
Claritin	10 mg	215.17	0.71	30,206
Keflex	250 mg	157.39	1.88	8,272
Lipitor	20 mg	272.37	5.80	4,596
Norvasc	10 mg	188.29	0.14	134,393
Prevacid	30 mg	344.77	1.01	34,036
Prilosec	20 mg	419.00	0.52	80,477
Prozac	20 mg	247.47	0.11	224,873
Tenormin	50 mg	104.47	0.13	80,262
Vasotec	10 mg	102.37	0.20	51,085
Xanax	1 mg	136.79	0.02	569,858
Zoloft	50 mg	206.87	1.75	11,721
Source: Life Extension Magazine, Mar.2005, p.11				

IS IT SAFE?

"Today we are faced with what may be the single greatest drug safety catastrophe in the history of this country or the history of the world... In my opinion, the FDA has let the American people down, and sadly, betrayed a public trust." **David Graham, MD, MPH, Associate Director of Drug Safety, Food and Drug Administration, Nov.2004**

The Food and Drug Administration (FDA) began its authoritarian rule of the American drug and supplement industry after the drug Thalidomide caused major birth deformities in 10,000 babies in Europe and Africa between 1956-62. No doubt that we need some form of policing to insure that our foods are safe and our drugs are safe and effective if used as directed. Our current government watch dog groups are incapable of doing this job. For example, Vioxx, a drug to reduce pain and inflammation, was associated with 100,000 unnecessary deaths during its use in 20 million people between 1999 and 2004. Since the FDA is primarily funded by fees paid by the pharmaceutical industry, conflicts of interest abound.

BAD MEDICINE?
"Beware the military industrial complex" Dwight Eisenhower, 34th president of USA.

And all of this cost and risk might be acceptable if Americans were healthier than other countries. We are not. In a detailed survey comparing the health care systems of America, United Kingdom, Australia, Canada, Germany, and New Zealand; America came in dead last, in spite of having the most expensive health care system. Australia came in first place. The World Health Organization (WHO), in 2000, ranked the U.S. health care system as the most expensive in the world, yet 37th in overall performance, and 72nd by overall level of health among the 191 nations included in the study.

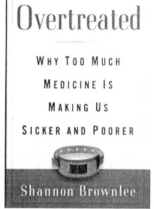

According to medical journalist, Shannon Brownlee, we spend roughly 1/3 or $700 billion annually for ineffective medical care, another $700 billion annually for dangerous counterproductive medical care, the remaining $700 billion for appropriate medical care.

General Motors, once the largest corporation in the world, is now bankrupt. GM insured 1.1 million employees and their dependents at a cost of $5.2 billion per year. On each car sold, $1400 went to health insurance for employees, which is more than they spent on steel for their cars. GM had $77 billion in future health care commitments with only $20 billion set aside for this purpose. Game over.

CANCER TREATMENT NEEDS REFORM

When Richard Nixon launched the "war on cancer" in December of 1971, he confidently proclaimed that we would have a cure for a major cancer within 5 years. Now, 38 years later, over $90 billion in public research funds spent at the National Cancer Institute, and over $1 trillion spent in therapy for cancer patients, we don't have any unqualified cures for any cancers. Five year survival rates for advanced breast and lung cancer are unchanged. In 1900 only 3% of deaths in America were caused by cancer. Today it's 24%. As of 2004, cancer is the number one cause of death in America.

The five year survival rate in 22 different cancers has been increased by 2.1% using chemotherapy, according to a review in the journal Clinical Oncology. That is not much of a benefit given the horrendous side effects, costs, and toxicities of chemo. Another study from the Buck Institute for Age Research found that chemo may promote the development of cancer later in life. "Chemotherapy is brutal..." according to the study's chair, Dr. Judith Campisi. In a 2008 study published in the Archives of Internal Medicine following 110,000 Norwegian women, researchers found that women who DID NOT get mammograms had 22% fewer breast cancers. Essentially, many breast lumps will spontaneously disappear and need not have dramatic invasive toxic oncology care. "Uncertainty about the value of mammography continues." wrote the editorial.

Of all drugs evaluated by Dr. Brian Spear in the scientific journal *Trends in Molecular Medicine*, cancer drugs were the least effective, being effective only 25% of the time, with pain medication (analgesics) the most effective at 80%. John Bailar, MD, PhD, former editor of the New England Journal of Medicine, called the war on cancer "a qualified failure". Yet, chemo, radiation and surgery are the only reimbursable therapies offered to most American cancer patients, who have to go to Germany or Mexico to find treatment options.

WHY WOULD ANYONE INSURE A BURNING BUILDING?

Many Americans are "arsonists" with their destructive lifestyle creating health problems that are treated in the most expensive and dangerous way possible, with prescription drugs to relieve the symptoms, rather than using lifestyle to change the underlying cause of the disease. Smoking quadruples the risk for lung cancer, emphysema, and pulmonary disease. Obesity quadruples the risk for type 2 diabetes and hypertension. United Kingdom is beginning to deny medical therapies for patients who make poor lifestyle choices.

Nearly all of the 20 million diabetics in America have a self-induced lifestyle component to their disease. 80% of heart disease risk is lifestyle induced. A Mediterranean diet can reduce the risk of heart attack by 70%, while the $14 billion we spend annually on cholesterol lowering drugs only cuts the risk by half that much.

Yet state and federal authorities rigorously patrol medical offices for any signs of deviating from "standard of care", meaning non-traditional therapies. James Carter, MD, DPH, has written a disturbing book, RACKETEERING IN MEDICINE, detailing the "witch hunt" to eliminate any medical practice that uses protocols outside of prescription medication and surgery.

FINANCIAL MELTDOWN OF MODERN MEDICINE

"No good deed goes unpunished." Anonymous

In the dark days of World War II, America was struggling to climb out of the decade of financial depression while fighting a war on two continents. Most able-bodied young men went to war. Women, like my grandmother, worked in the factories to provide supplies to the war movement. In order to prevent inflation, the federal government mandated wage freezes. Yet manufacturers had contracts with the government to produce airplanes, ships, and all the other needs of war. So employers started offering "free health care" as an incentive to bring capable workers to their factories. Seemed like an innocent idea at the time, but it has become a Pandora's box.

Once the war was over, the concept of free health care as a "perk" (perquisite) grew in popularity, especially among union jobs. Once Mom and Dad had free healthcare, the next step was getting free health care for Grandma and Grandpa, which began with the passage of the Medicare Act in 1965. We need to take care of our senior citizens. Yet America has lost the concept of "personal accountability" that founded this country and put us at the top of the world's caste system.

Medicare and Medicaid comprise a "debt that we cannot pay" or unsecured liability of around $62 trillion. We currently spend a billion dollars a day on Medicare, of which 60% goes to treat patients in their last 6 months of life, with questionable results in either quality or quantity of life. A Dartmouth study found that 30% of Medicare spending is wasted.

Health care costs have made America far less competitive in the global economy, resulting in millions of jobs "outsourced" overseas. Social Security and Medicare are already the largest expenses in the federal budget. The aging of the 75 million baby boomers threatens a "perfect financial storm", since people under 65 years of age use $2761 per year in medical services while those over 65 use $12,271, which is a 440% increase in medical use by the aged.

FREE MARKET SOLUTIONS?

Some experts say that the "free market" system could fix our problems. Let capitalism do its work in lowering costs and improving quality through free market competition. The plastic surgery field has led the way. Since plastic surgery is usually not insurance reimbursable, the industry had to compete for customers like any other segment of capitalism. The result over the past decade is a tripling of consumer use and an 84% drop in costs, all due to free market competition. Let the consumer pick and choose health care providers and therapies. Expand our options for treatment. Let "outcomes data" show us the most clinically effective and cost effective therapies. Costs will be controlled when the consumer has a vested interest in the game. Let the insurance actuarial use real risk calculation to assess health insurance. Let the government act as the "referee" in this business, making sure the "game" is played fairly.

If not free market, then let the government take over health care with a single payer system--nationalized health care. The Veteran's Health Administration, run by the government for veterans, has become a model of efficiency, treating patients for half the cost of other health care institutions, with a prescription accuracy rate of 99.9% and lower hospital infection rate. What we have now is some Frankenstein hybrid of health care that limits the free market considerably with a myriad of unnecessary governmental regulations and bureaucracies. Free market or government run. Take your pick. We could not do any worse than what we have right now.

WHOLE FOODS AND LIFESTYLE AS THE SOLUTION

This chapter was meant to open your eyes to our ineffective health care system. You are encouraged to work with your doctor and continue on your medication while changing your diet and lifestyle so that, hopefully, you do not need the medication.

Whole foods offer us a treasure chest of known nutrients and more obscure "conditionally essential" nutrients that may be able to dramatically bolster your body's ability to heal itself. And that is the best medicine of all.

PATIENT PROFILE: Benito Martinez Abrogan died in 2006 at the age of 120, leaving the oldest living human title to someone else. Mr.Abrogan was part of one of the poorest countries on earth, Cuba, which spends an average of $251 per person per year with free health care for all, compared to the $7900 per person in the United States providing patchy elitist coverage with dramatic invasive medicine as the prize. Cuba has so many centenarians (people who live to be 100) that they have a club. Mr. Abrogan lived a simple peasant's life: hard work daily, walked everywhere, only ate what he could raise which was a plant-food dominated diet. There are many books, including BLUE ZONES by Dan Buettner, which try to bring reason to the elusive subject of longevity. In general, the oldest people in the world work hard, live in the country away from city stress and pollution, eat a plant based organically grown diet, take naps, are respected for their age, no vaccinations, all breast fed as infants, have a sense of community in living with family and around friends, drink clean water that is high in minerals, and do not use medical services. Maybe our health care meltdown or metamorphosis will bring us a more sane, humane, scientific, and effective health care system.

ENDNOTES

[1] . Lazarou J, Pomeranz BH, Corey PN: "Incidence of adverse drug reactions in hospitalized patients." JAMA 1998;279:1200.

CHAPTER 4
THE LAWS OF OPTIMAL NUTRITION: DEVELOPING GOOD JUDGMENT

"Each patient carries his own doctor inside him. We are at our best when we give the doctor who resides within a chance to go to work."
Albert Schweitzer, MD, 1940, Nobel Laureate & medical missionary

FROM NATURE'S PHARMACY: THE BANANA BONANZA

Few foods can rival the bonanza of nutrition found in a banana. Available nearly everywhere nearly any time of the year. Comes in it own wrapper, like nature's zip lock bag for a day trip. Grown in over 100 tropical countries throughout the world, the banana is 75% water and 25% solids, including a decent source of vitamin C, A, B-6 and magnesium; and a fantastic source of potassium...a mineral in which Americans are chronically deficient. Bananas have a low glycemic index (do not dramatically raise blood glucose) and provide a nice boost of mental and physical energy. A medium banana has 108 kcal, 1 gram of protein, negligible fat, and a rich source of pectin, a soluble fiber that helps with regularity and lowering cholesterol levels in the blood. Bananas are a favorite folk remedy for mild depression, premenstrual syndrome, hangovers, heart burn, obesity, and ulcers; use the inside of the peelings applied topically to accelerate healing of bug bites and warts. The FDA agrees with the ability of bananas to help lower blood pressure with its mighty potassium content. The pectin in a banana provides the "frosting on the cake" for many of my blender drinks. Throw in whatever fruits and vegetables into your high speed blender, then blend in ½ peeled banana for that smooth texture and keeping everything in solution. Peel bananas and freeze in a zip lock bag. Use ½ frozen banana to give your blender drinks a cold milk shake-like mouth feel. Great on hot summer days!

NUTRITIONAL NAVIGATION

LEARNING
GOOD JUDGMENT
NUTRITIONAL
NAVIGATION

When sailing instructors teach you how to sail, they cannot show you around the world. They show you how to use the instruments of navigation-- a sextant, compass and map--and hope you can fare well on your own. The purpose of this chapter is to condense the volumes of nutrition information into several easy-to-follow rules that become your navigation instruments in choosing the right foods. I have tried giving patients a detailed 2 week food intake program. By day 2, this patient is out of some food, then eats with a friend at a restaurant, then has dinner with the cousins--all of which throws the patient off their diet without any idea of knowing how to "wing it" or improvise. Use this chapter as a shortcut toward building good nutrition judgment in choosing foods and supplements that will prevent disease and build good health.

>The KISS (keep it simple, student) method of optimal nutrition.

-Go natural. Eat foods in as close to their natural state as possible. Refining food often adds questionable agents (like food additives, salt, sugar and fat), removes valuable nutrients (like vitamins, minerals, and fiber) and always raises the cost of the food.

-Expand your horizons. Eat a wide variety of foods. By not focusing on any particular food, you can obtain nutrients that may be essential but are poorly understood while also avoiding a buildup of any substance that could create food allergies or toxicities.

-Nibbling is better. Eat small frequent meals. Nibbling is better than gorging. Our ancestors "grazed" throughout the day. Only with the advent of the industrial age did we begin the punctual eating of large meals. Nibbling helps to stabilize blood sugar levels and minimize insulin rushes; therefore has been linked to a lowered risk for heart disease, diabetes, obesity and mood swings.

-Seek out nutrient-dense foods. Maximize your intake of life-giving foods, including fresh vegetables, whole grains, legumes, fruit,

low fat meat (turkey, fish, chicken) and clean water. Low fat dairy products, especially yogurt, can be valuable if you do not have milk allergies or lactose intolerance.

 -Monitor your quality of weight, rather than quantity of weight. Balance your calorie intake with expenditure so that your percentage of body fat is reasonable. Pinch the skin fold just above the hipbone. If this skin is more than an inch in thickness, then you may need to begin rational efforts to lose weight. How much you weigh is not nearly as crucial as the percent of fat in the body. Most nutritionists agree that too much fat stored in the body (obesity) is a real killer. Buy a Tanita (Tanita.com) scale for measuring percent body fat.

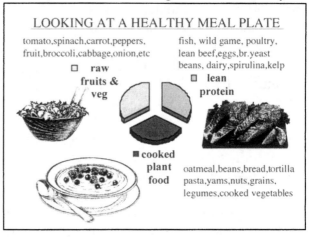

LOOKING AT A HEALTHY MEAL PLATE

raw fruits & veg — tomato,spinach,carrot,peppers, fruit,broccoli,cabbage,onion,etc

lean protein — fish, wild game, poultry, lean beef,eggs,br.yeast beans, dairy,spirulina,kelp

cooked plant food — oatmeal,beans,bread,tortilla pasta,yams,nuts,grains, legumes,cooked vegetables

 -Eat enough protein. Take in about 1 gram of protein for each kilogram of body weight. Example: 150 pound patient. Divide 150 pounds by 2.2 to find 68 kilograms, yields 68 grams of protein daily is needed to regenerate a healthy body.

 -Use supplements in addition to, rather than instead of, good food. Get your nutrients primarily with a fork and spoon. Do not place undo reliance on pills and powders to provide optimal nourishment while eating a poor diet. Supplements (such as ImmunoPower EZ, from GettingHealthier.com) can provide minerals that are missing in our diet, vitamins that are removed in processing, bolster our nutrient intake beyond "surviving" (RDA) into "thriving" levels, and help us to better tolerate the myriad of toxins found in our 21st century planet.

 -Shop the perimeter of grocery store. On the outside of your grocery store you will find fresh fruits, vegetables, bread, fish, chicken and dairy. Once you venture into the deep dark interior of the grocery store, nutritional quality of the foods goes way down and prices go way up. Organic produce is raised without pesticides and may be

valuable in helping certain sensitive individuals. However, organic produce is unavailable or unaffordable for many people. Don't get terribly concerned about having to consume organic produce. Any produce that cannot be peeled (like watermelon or bananas) should be soaked for 5 minutes in a solution of one gallon lukewarm clean water with 2 tablespoons of vinegar, which will remove pesticide residue.

-If a food will not rot or sprout, then don't buy it or throw it out. Your body cells have similar biochemical needs to a bacteria or yeast cell. Foods that have a shelf life of a millennium are not going to nourish the body. Think about it: if bacteria is not interested in your food, then what makes you think that your body cells are interested? Foods that cannot begin (sprouting) or sustain (bacterial growth) life elsewhere, will have a similar effect in your body.

-Dishes should be easy to clean. Foods that are hard to digest or unhealthy will probably leave a mess on plates and pots. Dairy curd, such as fondue, is both difficult to clean and very difficult for your stomach to process. Same thing with fried, greasy or burned foods.

>**Essential nutrient pyramid.**

We need to recognize the priority placed on essential nutrients. We can live weeks without food, a few days without water and only a few minutes without oxygen. Keep in mind the relative importance of these essential nutrients.

FOOD PYRAMID

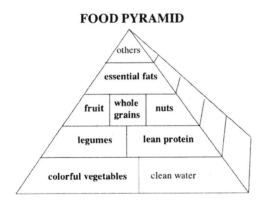

Oxygen and water form the basis of human life. Make sure that your quality and quantity of intake pay homage to this fact. Protein, carbohydrate, fiber and fat form the next level of importance. Vitamins and minerals are the essential micronutrients required for health.

Above these essential substances are two levels of quasi (meaning "as if it were") nutrients. Conditionally essential nutrients include Coenzyme-Q10, carnitine, EPA and GLA (fatty acids) and much more. Some people may require these nutrients in the diet during certain stressful phases of their lives. Minor dietary constituents (MDCs) include a wide variety of plant compounds that have shown remarkable anti-cancer and health-promoting abilities. Indoles in the cabbage family, lycopenes in tomatoes, allicin in garlic, immune stimulants in sea vegetables and others make up this new and exciting category. Eating a wide variety of unprocessed plant foods will help to insure adequate intake of these quasi-nutrients.

>**Expect the existence of unknown essential nutrients.**

As laboratory equipment becomes more sophisticated, we keep finding more substances in the food supply that can help or hurt us. Macronutrients, which are found in large amounts in the diet, were discovered first, and micronutrients second. An entire universe of "sub-micro" nutrients await us as we look at substances found in the food supply in parts per trillion. Not until laboratory equipment could detect pesticide residues and minor dietary constituents could we begin to appreciate their importance in health. If you asked a nutritionist in 1929 to talk about the importance of vitamin B-12 and selenium, they would have remarked "These nutrients don't exist, because we can't find them, therefore they aren't important." Similarly, there are "sub-nutrients" in whole food that are ignored today but will eventually be recognized for their important role in health.

For example, infant formulas were first tried 3000 years ago and became fashionable with the royalty in Europe in the past 500 years. By 1700 AD, it was recognized that feeding your child animal milk rather than human breast milk brought nearly a 90% mortality rate. "Wet nurses" were peasant women brought in to breastfeed the children of nobility. By 1950, scientists felt confident that they could duplicate and even improve on breast milk. They were wrong. Since then, we have learned of the special fatty acids (EPA & GLA) contained in breast milk for brain development, the amino acid taurine for brain and sight, immunoglobulins that share mother's acquired immunity with the newborn infant, substances that help mature the intestinal lining and the pancreatic cells, and much more.

Studies show that breastfed infants later in life are at lower risk for heart disease, diabetes, allergies, sudden infant death (SID) and even emotional problems. Still, breastfeeding is only beginning to make a comeback, with less than 20% of American mothers nursing their young. We thought that we could duplicate mother's milk, but we really didn't understand the elegant symphony of "sub-micro" nutrients that it contained. Same applies with our foods. The more that we tamper with our food supply, the more hard lessons we learn regarding the ornate and subtle blend of potent nutrients offered by nature.

>Difference between surviving and thriving.

Recognize the difference between surviving and thriving. Half of the people on earth live at or near poverty level. They survive. They do not thrive. Similarly, there are biochemical levels of nutrients in the body that allow us to thrive rather than just survive.

Humans have survived car crashes at 200 miles per hour, falling out of jet planes without a parachute from five miles up, being fired out of cannons, inhumane treatment in prisoner of war camps, multiple gun shot wounds and a metal shaft fired cleanly through the head. While some people can survive a half century of smoking, no one thrives on it. Alcoholics can tolerate a suicidal lifestyle for decades. But their body and mind suffer and age rapidly in the process. None of these feats are good for the human body. Yet our tenacity is oftentimes our undoing. We assume that a diet that doesn't immediately kill us must be good for us. Not so.

The statistical picture of the average American is indicative of a tenacious survivor: overweight; 6 colds per year; chronic mild depression, constipation, and lethargy; dentures by age 45, chronic illness by age 60 with 6 different daily drugs needed; and death in the 70s from heart

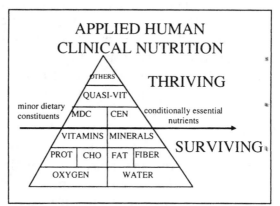

disease or cancer. None of this would be considered thriving--nor is our lifestyle "optimal".

We need to pursue optimal health and "thriving" before our many ailments will go away. There appears to be a "dose-dependent" response curve with the health benefits of many nutrients.

Think of the benefits of increasing daily intake of folate:

-Most people can live on 100 micrograms (mcg)

-Wound healing and overall health are improved at 400 mcg

-The risk for pregnant women having babies with neural tubes defect can be lowered dramatically at 1000 mcg

-Pre-cancerous conditions of the cervix and lungs can be reversed with 20,000 mcg.

Most people can survive for decades on 10 international units (iu) of vitamin E. Yet, 100 iu of E will improve lung resistance to air pollutants and lower the risk for heart disease, while 800 iu has been shown to measurably elevate immune functions. Humans can survive on 10 milligrams (mg) of vitamin C for decades. Yet, many experts recommend 400 mg as a healthier RDA, and 10,000 mg helps to fight AIDS, cancer and the flu. In a study reported by UCLA researchers, 300 mg of supplemental vitamin C daily lengthened lifespan in men by 6 years.[1] Clearly, survival levels of nutrient intake are not enough for the person who wants to thrive. Intake of whole foods helps to elevate us beyond surviving into thriving.

>**Simple solutions for complex problems.**

Most medical therapies have been serious disappointments in treating degenerative diseases, including heart disease, cancer, stroke, arthritis, diabetes, osteoporosis, Alzheimer's disease and more. After decades of work from brilliants scientists, there is always another unexpected obstacle around the bend that leads to toxic side effects and reduced therapeutic value from most medications or surgical procedures. The reason for these frustrating results is our arrogance. We assume that we fully understand the interdependent and complex machinery of the human body. Yet we have only a vague grasp of how to optimally support the mind and body. We dump billions of pounds of known lethal poisons in our air, food and water supply; then subject ourselves to unprecedented levels of psychological distress; then fill our stomachs with nutritionally bankrupt food. When our health fails, we cut off the defective part or try some dramatic, invasive, expensive therapy that will combat the disease. Somehow, we ignore the obvious and easy answers. The solution to many health problems revolves around nourishing our own internal healing ability--the "life forces" within.

>The treatment of degenerative disease must deal with the cause.

The same lifestyle factors which prevent heart disease--stress reduction (meditation), walking and a low fat plant-based diet--can also reverse heart disease, as demonstrated by Dr. Dean Ornish. If your headache is caused by your teenager's drums, then no amount of aspirin, antacid, or tranquilizers will actually cure the problem until you stop the noise. Drugs and surgery can provide temporary relief from symptoms, but cannot reverse the underlying mechanisms that brought about the disease. If a long term zinc deficiency blunted the immune   system,   which   led

ETIOLOGY FOR MOST DISEASES
pull out the weed by the root

primary etiology	secondary etiology	diagnosed diseases
NUTRITION	INFECTIONS	HEART DISEASE
INFECTIONS	INFLAMMATION	CANCER
EXERCISE	HYPERCOAGUL	DIABETES
ATTITUDE	DYSBIOSIS	STROKE
TOXINS	HYPOTHYROID	AUTO-IMMUNE
ENERGY ALIGN	MALDIGESTION	CHRONIC FATIG
GENETIC VULN	IMMUNE DYSFUN	MENTAL ILLNESS
	HYPERGLYCEMIA	ALZHEIMER'S
	ALLERGIES	PARKINSON'S
	HORMONE IMBAL	et al.
	OXIDATIVE STRES	
	ACIDOSIS	

to cancer; then only zinc supplements can reverse the condition. If a painful divorce caused depression which blunted the immune system, then resolution of the psychological stress is the only long term cure. If low thyroid output is the problem that led to cancer, then normalizing thyroid is the answer. For most Americans, disease is a result of many combined negative forces. Pure and simple: reverse the cause and you have a much better chance for a cure.

>Biochemical individuality--we are all different.

Stroll through a big city zoo if you want to truly appreciate the diversity of life on earth. There are creatures that eat mostly meat, like cats, who would die on a vegetarian diet. There are creatures, like elephants and rabbits, that are strict vegetarians and would die on a carnivorous diet. There are many shades of gray in between these two extremes, like omnivorous humans. The five billion people on the planet earth comprise an incredible tapestry of biochemical and physical diversity. Eskimos eat a diet primarily composed of high fat fish, with almost no fruit, vegetables, or fiber to speak of. Yet they are an incredibly hardy group of people, nearly devoid of heart disease, cancer or diabetes. They are eating their "factory specification" diet to which they have adapted.

Our ancestors of 5000 years ago were mostly hunters and gathers. In colder climates, such as northern Europe, plant food was only available throughout the summer and fall. Lean wild game and fish provided the bulk of food intake throughout winter. In warmer climates, like central Africa and India, the inhabitants relied on a year round diet of mostly fresh plant food. There are many shades of dietary needs in between these extremes. The take home lesson here is: "eat what you are supposed to eat from your ancient heritage." As ethnic groups blend in marriage, this "ancestral diet" becomes a more complex issue with our mixed racial backgrounds.

>Nutrients as biological response modifiers (BRM).

About 30 young American men die each year during early football season from dehydration. Large men out of shape working hard in the late summer heat and not drinking enough water all makes for a dangerous situation referred to as "heat stroke". It can be lethal. The only cure is water. Water becomes a blatant biological response modifier in this case. But all foods that we eat have similarities to this situation because food and drink change the way the body works--for better or worse.

Most Americans choose their food for reasons of taste, cost, convenience and psychological gratification. All those reasons are okay, as long as we do not forget the real reason that we eat: to nourish the cells of the body with essential ingredients from the diet. Every time you eat, picture the cavalry from the old west delivering the long-awaited supplies to fort--you better have the right stuff with you. While humans can survive on many different bad diets for years, we can only thrive on a narrowly defined set of nutrition principles.

Know this rule: everything that you put in your mouth is a BRM. Brilliant scientists at the National Cancer Institute have labored for years trying to produce something from the laboratory that will rectify human cancer. These researchers have developed the field of BRM, in which potent drugs and extracts from the immune system will hopefully improve health. Results in this area have been very disappointing.

But every time you eat a meal high in carbohydrates and get a little sleepy afterward, you have used food as a BRM to alter brain chemicals. A high salt diet changes the critical sodium to potassium ratio in the blood and cell membranes, which can affect many

NUTRIENTS AS BIOLOGICAL RESPONSE MODIFIERS
Self-regulatory mechanisms; feeding homeostasis
The ability or tendency of an organism or a cell to maintain
internal equilibrium by adjusting its physiological processes.
"Non-specific host defense mechanisms"

➔IMMUNE REGULATORS
➔ALTER GENETIC EXPRESSION
➔CELL MEMBRANE DYNAMICS
➔DETOXIFICATION
➔PH MAINTENANCE, BALANCING PROTONS
➔PROOXIDANTS & AOX, BALANCING ELECTRONS
➔CELLULAR COMMUNICATIONS (signal cell transduction)
➔PROSTAGLANDIN REGULATION
➔STEROID HORMONE CONTROL
➔ENERGY METABOLISM: AEROBIC VS ANAEROBIC
➔PROBIOTICS VS DYSBIOSIS
➔ANTI-PROLIFERATIVE AGENTS

hormones and the permeability of cell membranes. Respect the incredible impact of food, water and air on the mind and body.
>**All lifestyle factors are health vectors.**

Vectors are forces, which vary in strength and direction. For instance, a small plane flying at 100 miles per hour north into a head wind at 120 mph has a ground speed of -20 mph. Progress is seriously impaired by the opposing force of the wind.

All lifestyle factors are vectors which either move you toward illness or wellness. Consider the person who is smoking (-80 mph), eats a low fat diet (+60 mph), takes vitamin supplements (+40 mph), has a stressful attitude (-100 mph), and eats a high sugar diet ((-80). The overwhelming direction for this person is toward illness, even though he or she is doing some things right. Health is a sum total of vectors. For optimal health, get all vectors heading in a favorable direction.

>**The more wellness you have, the less illness you can have.**

Just like darkness is the absence of light, disease is the absence of wellness. Wellness is a state of optimal functioning of body, mind and spirit. A well person may have 90% wellness and 10% illness. A sick person may have 10% wellness and 90% illness. A body region cannot be well and ill at the same time. Therefore, curing illness is a matter of replacing it with wellness. The same unhealthy lifestyle may create heart disease in 30% of the people, cancer in 25%, arthritis in 10%, and mental illness in 5%. In a very important step toward removing illness, simply allow wellness to infiltrate the body and mind.

IMMUNE SYSTEM

- Enhanced by:
- Vitamins: A, C, E, B-6
- Minerals: Zn, Cr, Se
- Quasi-vit: CoQ, EPA, GLA
- Amino acids: arg, gluta
- Herbals: astragalus, Cat's claw, Pau D'arco
- Foods: yogurt, cartilage, garlic, enzymes, green leafy, shark oil, colostrum
- Positive emotions: love

- Reduced by:
- Toxic metals: Cd, Pb, Hg
- VOC: PCB, benzene
- Sugar: glycemic index
- Omega 3:6 ratio, 1:1; 1:16
- Stress: depression

>Build your immune defenses through diet, exercise and lifestyle.

We have an extensive network of protective factors that circulate throughout our bodies to kill any bacteria, virus, yeast or cancer cells. Think of these 20 trillion immune cells as both your Department of Defense and your waste disposal company. Cells in your body are duplicating all day every day at a blinding pace. This process of growth is fraught with peril. When cells are not copied exactly as they should be, then an emergency call goes out to the immune system to find and destroy this abnormal saboteur cell. This process occurs frequently in most people throughout their lives. Nearly half, or 42% of Americans can expect to develop cancer in their lifetime, yet most experts agree that everyone gets cancer about 6 times per lifetime. Same with infections. We are constantly bombarded with pathogens from our air, food, and water; yet it is the surveillance of an alert and capable immune system that defends most of us from cancer, infections, and premature aging.

DOES SALT CAUSE HIGH BLOOD PRESSURE?

There is some evidence that a high sodium (salt) diet causes high blood pressure in a minority of people. Yet, all of our body cells are bathed in a salty solution like the ocean. There is even more evidence that hypertension (high blood pressure) is much more complicated than monitoring salt intake. Fish oil (containing valuable omega 3 fats), vitamin C, calcium, magnesium, potassium, fitness, stress, body weight and percent body fat all add up to a complete equation that dictates hypertension. In general, animal foods are higher in sodium and plant foods are higher in potassium. Most people get enough salt without salting their food. However, intense perspiration through heat and exercise drains the body of salt through sweat. Make sure that you get enough calcium, magnesium, potassium and fish oil. Salt to taste. Monitor your blood pressure. The vast majority of the population can eat reasonable amounts of salt without measurable increases in blood pressure. See the included pull out chart for options on salty condiments: miso, Lite salt (half sodium, half potassium), vinegar, kelp, lemon juice, and more.

RAW OR COOKED FOOD?

All creatures on earth, except humans, eat exclusively raw food. Biologists tell us that humans began cooking their food around

400,000 years ago. Based upon these facts, some groups have decided to become "raw food" enthusiasts. To be sure, there are some merits in eating some foods raw. Fruits are best raw. Some vegetables, like carrots can be eaten raw. However, cooking food has the advantage of making foods easier to chew and digest while also neutralizing many bacteria, fungus, and parasites that are competing for our food supply. Some raw food, like potatoes, legumes, and grains, provide the body with nothing more than fiber unless cooked or sprouted. The net amount of calories derived from cooked foods is much higher than the calories from raw food, because the body has to work harder to break down complex molecules in raw food to derive nutritional benefit.

While the human brain comprises 5% of our body weight, it consumes 25% of the oxygen and calories. Human intelligence allowed humans to dominate the planet earth and adapt to rapidly changing environments. In a compelling paper presented by Richard Wrangham, PhD of Harvard University at the 2009 conference of the American Association for the Advancement of Science, Dr. Wrangham proposes that in order for humans to evolve, they needed cooked food as the "killer application (reference to quality computer software)" as the crucial link in maintaining our hungry brains. For the best of both raw and cooked food worlds, cover 1/3 of your dinner plate with cooked wholesome plant food (like oatmeal and steamed vegetables), 1/3 with cooked lean protein food (like turkey, salmon, eggs), and the remaining 1/3 with raw fruits and vegetables.

PRACTICING HERBAL MEDICINE WITHOUT A LICENSE

Our ancestors used herbal medicine as a primary form of preventive and curative therapies. The vast majority of the world still uses herbal medicine as its primary or only form of healing. That would make our current American allopathic system of patent drug use "alternative medicine", since we are in the minority of the world's people.

HERBAL MEDICINE

AS SUPPLEMENTS:	AS FOODS:	AS SEASONINGS:
echinacea	soy	garlic
astragalus	green & orange	onion
Cat's claw	dandelion greens	hot peppers
Pau D'arco	citrus	cinnamon
ginseng	tomato	ginger
grape seed extract	green tea	real licorice
aloe vera	broccoli/cabbage	turmeric (curry)
red clover	beets	parsley
milk thistle	sprouts	sage
Essiac	flaxseed meal	chicory
Hoxsey	sesame seeds	thyme
Flor-Essence	Maitake mushrm	basil

Herbal medicine starts in the kitchen with seasoning herbs that have been time tested for their safety and good taste while being scientifically validated for their ability to favorably alter the body's biochemistry. Enjoy!

PATIENT PROFILE: Surviving asbestos cancer. K.F. was diagnosed with mesothelioma, having spent some time in his youth working with asbestos. His original oncologist gave him an optimistic 6 months to live. He and his wife began using an aggressive diet and supplement program in conjunction with his chemotherapy. Three years later, K.F. still has the cancer, but has had an excellent quality of life and looks better than his neighbors. Nutrition doesn't cure every cancer patient, but it usually provides a dramatic extension in quality and quantity of life.

ENDNOTES

[1]. Enstrom, J., Epidemiology, vol.3, p.194, May 1992

CHAPTER 5
HEALTH BENEFITS
OF WHOLE FOODS

"Climb the mountains and get their good tidings. Nature's peace will flow into you as sunshine flows into trees. The winds will blow their own freshness into you, and the storms their energy, while cares will drop off like autumn leaves." John Muir, co-founder of national parks

FROM NATURE'S PHARMACY: lycopenes
You can imagine the surprise of the researchers when they discovered that people who ate more pizza had a lower risk of prostate cancer. The researchers isolated the "active ingredient" as lycopene, which is a red pigment found in tomatoes, watermelon, red grapefruit, papaya, and red peppers. Lycopenes help plants with photosynthesis, or gathering energy from the sun. Lycopenes in humans seem to have an ability to fight oxidation and possibly lower cancer risk and damage to the eyes and other tissue, thus slowing the aging process.[1] Cooking the tomatoes or adding oil (like olive oil) improves bioavailability.[2]

For the first 5000 years of civilization, humans relied on foods and herbs for medicine. Only in the past 50 years have we forgotten our medicinal "roots" in favor of patent medicines. While pharmaceuticals have their value, we should not forget the well-documented, non-toxic and inexpensive healing properties of whole foods.

Whole foods contain an elegant "symphony" of ingredients that we have only begun to appreciate due to the increasing sensitivity of our analytical equipment. The more that we analyze whole foods, the more we stand back with awe.

WHOLE FOODS OR FOOD REMNANTS?

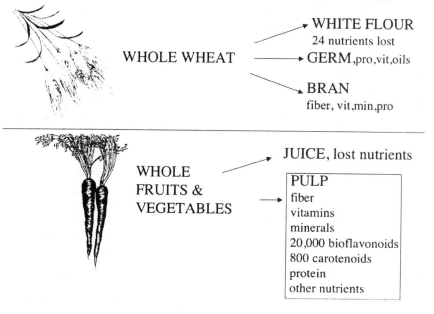

WHOLE WHEAT

→ WHITE FLOUR
24 nutrients lost

→ GERM,pro,vit,oils

→ BRAN
fiber, vit,min,pro

WHOLE FRUITS & VEGETABLES

→ JUICE, lost nutrients

→ PULP
fiber
vitamins
minerals
20,000 bioflavonoids
800 carotenoids
protein
other nutrients

The following list is but a sampling of the health benefits from whole foods. For more information see:
>HEALING POWER OF FOODS by Dr. Michael Murray
>FOOD: YOUR MIRACLE MEDICINE by Jean Carper
>HEALING FOODS by Patti Hausman, MS
-Apple. Lowers cholesterol and risk for cancer. Has mild antibacterial, antiviral, anti-inflammatory, estrogenic activity. High in fiber, helps avoid constipation, suppresses appetite. Juice can cause diarrhea in children.
　　-Asparagus. A super source of the antioxidant, glutathione to lower cancer risk.
　　-Avocado. Benefits circulation, lowers cholesterol, dilates blood vessels. Its main fat, monounsaturated oleic acid (also concentrated in olive oil), acts as an antioxidant to block artery-destroying toxicity of bad-type LDL cholesterol. One of the richest sources of glutathione, a powerful antioxidant, shown to block thirty

different carcinogens and to block proliferation of the AIDS virus in test tube experiments.

-Banana and Plantain. Soothes the stomach. Good for dyspepsia (upset stomach). Strengthens the stomach lining against acid and ulcers. Has antibiotic activity.

-Barley. Long known as a "heart medicine" in the Middle East. Reduces cholesterol. Has antiviral and anticancer activity. Contains potent antioxidants, including tocotrienols.

-Beans (legumes, including navy, black, kidney, pinto, soy beans and lentils). Potent medicine in lowering cholesterol. One-half cup of cooked beans daily reduces cholesterol an average 10 percent. Regulates blood sugar levels. An excellent food for diabetics. Linked to lower rates of certain cancers. Very high in fiber. A leading producer of intestinal gas in most people.

-Bell Pepper. Rich in antioxidant vitamin C. Helps to fight off colds, asthma, bronchitis, respiratory infections, cataracts, macular degeneration, angina, atherosclerosis and cancer.

-Blueberry. Acts as an unusual type antibiotic by blocking attachment of bacteria that cause urinary tract infections. Contains chemicals that curb diarrhea. Also antiviral activity and high in natural aspirin. Contains powerful antioxidants that may protect the back of the eye (retina) from damage, hence preserving healthy vision.

-Broccoli. A unique package of versatile disease-fighters. Abundant in antioxidants, including quercetin, glutathione, beta carotene, indoles, vitamin C, lutein, glucarate, sulforaphane. Extremely high anti-cancer activity, particularly against lung, colon and breast cancers. Like other cruciferous vegetables, it speeds up removal of estrogen from the body, helping suppress breast cancer. Rich in cholesterol-reducing fiber. Has antiviral, anti-ulcer activity. A super source of chromium that helps regulate insulin and blood sugar. Note: cooking and processing destroys some of the antioxidants and anti-estrogenic agents, such as indoles and glutathione. Most protective when eaten raw or lightly cooked.

-Brussels Sprouts. Cruciferous family possesses some of the same powers as broccoli and cabbage. Definitely anti-cancer, estrogenic and packed with various antioxidants and indoles.

-Cabbage (including bok choy). Revered in ancient Rome as a cancer cure. Contains numerous anticancer and antioxidant compounds. Speeds up estrogen metabolism, is thought to help block breast cancer and suppress growth of polyps, a prelude to colon cancer. Eating cabbage more than once a week cut men's colon cancer odds 66 percent. As little as two daily tablespoons of cooked cabbage protected against stomach cancer. Contains anti-ulcer compounds; cabbage juice helps heal ulcers in humans. Has antibacterial and anti-viral powers. Can cause flatulence in some. Some of these important compounds are destroyed by cooking. Raw cabbage, as in coleslaw, appears to have stronger overall health value.

-Carrot. A super source of beta carotene, a powerful anticancer, artery-protecting, immune-boosting, infection-fighting antioxidant with wide protective powers. A carrot a day slashed stroke rates in women by 68 percent. One medium carrot's worth of beta carotene cuts lung cancer risk in half, even among formerly heavy smokers. High doses of beta carotene, as found in carrots, substantially reduces odds of degenerative eye diseases (cataracts and macular degeneration) as well as chest pain (angina). Carrots' high soluble fiber depresses blood cholesterol, promotes regularity. Cooking can make it easier for the body to absorb beta carotene.

-Cauliflower. Cruciferous family member that contains many of the same cancer-fighting, hormone-regulating compounds as its cousins, broccoli and cabbage. Specifically thought to help ward off breast and colon cancers. Eat raw or lightly steamed.

-Celery. A traditional Vietnamese remedy for high blood pressure. Celery compounds reduce blood pressure in animals. Comparable human dose: two to four stalks a day. Also has a mild diuretic effect. Contains eight different families of anticancer compounds, such as phthalides and polyacetylenes, that detoxify carcinogens, especially cigarette smoke. Eating celery before or after vigorous exercise can induce mild to serious allergic reactions in some.

-Chili Pepper. Helps dissolve blood clots, opens up sinuses and air passages, breaks up mucus in the lungs, acts as an expectorant or decongestant, helps prevent bronchitis, emphysema and stomach ulcers. Most of chili pepper's pharmacological activity is credited to capsaicin (from the Latin "to bite"), the compound that makes the pepper taste hot. Also a potent painkiller, alleviating headaches when inhaled, and joint pain when injected. Hot paprika made from hot chili peppers is high in natural aspirin. Antibacterial, antioxidant activity. Putting hot chili sauce on food also speeds up metabolism, burning off calories. Chili peppers do not harm the stomach lining or promote ulcers.

-Chocolate. Contains chemicals thought to affect neurotransmitters in the brain. Added to milk, chocolate helps counteract lactose intolerance. Chocolate does not seem to raise cholesterol. Dark chocolate is high in copper and cacao (an antioxidant), which may help ward off cardiovascular disease. May trigger headaches or heartburn in some. Implicated in cystic breast disease. Choose chocolates that are 60% cacao and above.

-Cinnamon. A strong stimulator of insulin activity, thus potentially helpful for those with Type II diabetes. Mild anticoagulant activity.

-Clove. Used to kill the pain of toothache and as an anti-inflammatory against rheumatic diseases. Has anticoagulant effects, (anti-platelet aggregation), and its main ingredient, eugenol, is anti-inflammatory.

-Coffee. Most, but not all, of coffee's pharmacological impact comes from its high concentration of caffeine, a psychoactive drug. Caffeine, depending on an individual's biological makeup and peculiar sensitivity, can be a mood elevator and mental energizer. Improves mental performance in some. An emergency remedy for asthma. Dilates bronchial passages. Mildly addictive. Triggers headaches, anxiety and panic attacks in some. In excess may cause psychiatric disturbances. Promotes insomnia. Coffee stimulates stomach acid secretion (both caffeinated and decaf). Can aggravate heartburn. Promotes bowel movements in many, causes diarrhea in others. Caffeine may promote fibrocystic breast disease in some women.

-Collard Greens. Full of anticancer, antioxidant compounds, including lutein, vitamin C, beta carotene. In animals blocks the spread of breast cancer. Like other green leafy vegetables, associated with low rates of all cancers.

-Corn. Anticancer and antiviral activity, possibly induced by corn's content of protease inhibitors. Has estrogen-boosting capabilities. A very common cause of food intolerance linked to symptoms of rheumatoid arthritis, irritable bowel syndrome, headaches and migraine-related epilepsy in children.

-Cranberry. Strong antibiotic properties with unusual abilities to prevent infectious bacteria from sticking to cells lining the bladder and urinary tract. Thus, it helps prevent recurring urinary tract (bladder) infections. Also has antiviral activity.

-Date. High in natural aspirin. Has laxative effect. Dried fruits, including dates, are linked to lower rates of certain cancers, especially pancreatic cancer. Contains compounds that may cause headaches in susceptible individuals.

-Eggplant. Eggplant substances called glycoalkaloids, made into a topical cream medication, have been used to treat skin cancers such as basal cell carcinoma, according to Australian researchers. Also, eating eggplant may lower blood  cholesterol and help counteract some detrimental blood effects of fatty foods. Eggplant also has antibacterial and diuretic properties.

-Fenugreek Seeds. A spice common in the Middle East and available in many U.S. food markets. Has anti-diabetic powers. Helps control surges of blood sugar and insulin. Also anti-diarrhea, anti-ulcer, anti-diabetic, anticancer, tends to lower blood pressure, helps prevent intestinal gas.

-Fig. Helps to prevent cancer. Both extract of figs and the fig compound benzaldehyde have helped shrink tumors in humans, according to Japanese tests. Also laxative, anti-ulcer, antibacterial and anti-parasitic powers. Triggers headaches in some people.

-Fish and Fish Oil. An ounce a day has been shown to cut risk of heart attacks 50 percent. Oil in fish can relieve symptoms of rheumatoid arthritis, osteoarthritis, asthma, psoriasis, high blood pressure, Raynaud's disease, migraine headaches, ulcerative colitis, possibly multiple sclerosis. May help ward off strokes. A known anti-inflammatory agent and anticoagulant. Raises good type HDL cholesterol. Lowers triglycerides. Guard against glucose intolerance and Type II diabetes. Some fish are high in antioxidants, such as selenium and Coenzyme Q-10. Exhibits anticancer activity especially in blocking development of colon cancer and spread of breast cancer. Fish highest in omega-3 fatty acids include sardines, mackerel, herring, salmon, tuna.

-Garlic. Used to treat an array of ills since the dawn of civilization. Broad-spectrum antibiotic that combats bacteria, intestinal parasites and viruses. In high doses it has cured encephalitis. Lowers blood pressure and blood cholesterol, discourages dangerous blood clotting. Two or three cloves a day cut the odds of subsequent heart attacks in half in heart patients. Contains multiple anticancer compounds and antioxidants and tops the National Cancer Institute's list as a potential cancer-preventive food. Lessens chances of stomach cancer in particular. A good cold medication. Acts as a decongestant, expectorant, antispasmodic, anti-inflammatory agent. Boosts immune responses. Helps relieve gas, has anti-diarrhea, estrogenic and diuretic activity. Appears to lift mood and has a mild calming effect. High doses of *raw* garlic (more than three cloves a day) have caused gas, bloating, diarrhea and fever in some. Aged garlic may be better than cooked garlic. Eat garlic both raw and cooked for all-around insurance.

-Ginger. Used to treat nausea, vomiting, headaches, chest congestion, cholera, colds, diarrhea, stomach ache, rheumatism, and nervous diseases. Ginger is a proven anti-nausea, anti-motion sickness remedy that matches or surpasses drugs such as Dramamine. Helps thwart and prevent migraine headaches and osteoarthritis. Relieves symptoms of rheumatoid arthritis. Acts as an anti-thrombotic and anti-inflammatory agent in humans; is an antibiotic in test tubes (kills salmonella and staph bacteria), and an anti-ulcer agent in animals. Also, has anti-depressant, anti-diarrhea and strong antioxidant activity. High in anticancer activity.

-Grape. Rich in antioxidant compounds. Red grapes (but not white or green grapes), are high in antioxidant quercetin. Grape skins contain resveratrol, shown to inhibit blood-platelet clumping (and consequently, blood clot formation) and boost good-type HDL cholesterol. Red grapes are antibacterial and antiviral in test tubes. Grapeseed oil also raises good-type HDL cholesterol.

-Grapefruit. The pulp contains a unique pectin (in membranes and juice sacs—not in juice) that lowers blood cholesterol and reverses atherosclerosis (clogged arteries) in animals. Has anticancer activity, and appears particularly protective against stomach and pancreatic cancer. The juice is antiviral. High in various antioxidants, especially vitamin C. Helps with weight loss.

-Honey. Strong antibiotic properties. Has sleep-inducing sedative and tranquilizing properties.

-Kale. Rich source of various anticancer chemicals. Has more beta carotene than spinach and twice as much lutein, the most of any vegetable tested. Kale is also a member of the cruciferous family, endowing it with anticancer indoles that help regulate estrogen and fight off colon cancer.

-Kiwi Fruit. Commonly prescribed in Chinese traditional medicine to treat stomach and breast cancer. High in vitamin C.

-Licorice. Strong anticancer powers, possibly because of a high concentration of glycyrrhizin. Mice drinking glycyrrhizin dissolved in water have fewer skin cancers. Also kills bacteria, fights ulcers and diarrhea. May act as a diuretic. Too much licorice can raise blood pressure. Also it is not advised for pregnant women. Only real licorice has these powers. Licorice "candy" sold in the United States is made with anise instead of real licorice. Real licorice says "licorice mass." Imitation licorice is labeled "artificial licorice" or "anise."

-Melon (green and yellow, such as cantaloupe and honeydew). Has anticoagulant (blood-thinning) activity. Contain antioxidant beta carotene.

-Milk. Cancer-fighting powers, possibly against colon, lung, stomach and cervical cancers, especially in low-fat milk. One study detected less cancer among low-fat milk drinkers than non-milk drinkers. May help prevent high blood pressure. Skim milk may lower blood cholesterol. Milk fat promotes cancer and heart disease.
Milk is also an unappreciated terror in triggering "allergic" reactions that induce joint pain and symptoms of rheumatoid arthritis, asthma, irritable bowel syndrome and diarrhea. In children and infants milk is suspected to cause or contribute to colic, respiratory problems, sleeplessness, itchy rashes, migraines, epileptic seizures, ear infections and even diabetes. May retard healing of ulcers.

-Mushroom (Asian, including shiitake). A longevity tonic, heart medicine and cancer remedy in Asia. Current tests show mushrooms, such as Maitake, help prevent and/or treat cancer, viral diseases, such as influenza and polio, high blood cholesterol, sticky blood platelets and high blood pressure. Eaten daily, Maitake or shiitake, fresh (three ounces) or dried (one-third ounce) cut cholesterol by 7 and 12 percent respectively. A shiitake compound, lentinan, is a broad-spectrum antiviral agent that potentiates immune functioning. Used to treat leukemia in China and breast cancer in Japan. Extract (sulfated B-glucans) has been declared by Japanese scientists more effective as an AIDS drug than the common drug AZT. Eating black ("tree ear") mushroom "thins the blood." No therapeutic effects are known for the common U.S. button mushroom. Some claim this species has cancer-causing potential (hydrazides) unless cooked.

-Mustard (including horseradish). Recognized for centuries as a decongestant and expectorant. Helps break up mucus in air passages. A good remedy for congestion caused by colds and sinus problems. Also antibacterial. Increases metabolism, burning off extra calories. In one British test about three-fifths of a teaspoon of ordinary yellow mustard increased metabolic rate about 25 percent, burning forty-five more calories in three hours.

-Nuts. Anticancer and heart-protective properties. A key food among Seventh-Day Adventists, known for their low rates of heart disease. Walnuts and almonds help reduce cholesterol, contain high concentrations of antioxidant oleic acid and monounsaturated fat, similar to that in olive oil, known to protect arteries from damage. Nuts generally are high in antioxidant vitamin E, shown to protect against chest pain and artery damage. Brazil  nuts are extremely rich in selenium, an antioxidant linked to lower rates of heart disease and cancer. Walnuts contain ellagic acid, an antioxidant and cancer-fighter, and are also high in omega-3 type oil. Nuts, including peanuts, are good regulators of insulin and blood sugar, preventing steep rises, making them good foods for those with glucose intolerance and diabetes. Peanuts also are estrogenic. Nuts have been found lacking in the diets of those who later develop

Parkinson's disease. Prime cause of acute allergic reactions in susceptible individuals.

-Oats. Can depress cholesterol 10 percent or more, depending on individual responses. Oats help stabilize blood sugar, have estrogenic and antioxidant activity. They also contain psychoactive compounds that may combat nicotine cravings and have antidepressant powers. High doses can cause gas, abdominal bloating and pain in some.

-Olive oil. Lowers bad LDL cholesterol without lowering good HDL cholesterol. Helps keep bad cholesterol from being converted to a toxic or "oxidized" form. Thus, helps protect arteries from plaque. Reduces blood pressure, helps regulate blood sugar. Has potent antioxidant activity. Best oil for kitchen cooking and salads.

-Onion (including chives, shallots, scallions, leeks). Reputed in ancient Mesopotamia to cure virtually everything. An exceptionally strong antioxidant. Full of numerous anticancer agents. Blocks cancer dramatically in animals. The onion is the richest dietary source of quercetin, a potent antioxidant (in shallots, yellow and red onions  only—not white onions). Specifically linked to inhibiting human stomach cancer. Thins the blood, lowers cholesterol, raises good-type HDL cholesterol (preferred dose: half a raw onion a day), wards off blood clots, fights asthma, chronic bronchitis, hay fever, diabetes, atherosclerosis and infections. Anti-inflammatory, antibiotic, antiviral, thought to have diverse anticancer powers. Quercetin is also a sedative. Onions aggravate heartburn, may promote gas.

-Orange. Natural cancer-inhibitor, includes carotenoids, terpenes and flavonoids. Also rich in antioxidant vitamin C and beta carotene. Specifically tied to lower rates of pancreatic cancer. Orange juice protected mice sperm from radiation damage. Because of its high vitamin C, oranges may help ward off asthma attacks, bronchitis, breast cancer, stomach cancer, atherosclerosis, gum disease, and boost fertility and healthy sperm in some men. May aggravate heartburn.

-Parsley. Anticancer because of its high concentrations of antioxidants, such as monoterpenes, phthalides, polyacetylenes. Can help detoxify carcinogens and neutralize certain carcinogens in tobacco smoke. Also, has diuretic activity.

-Pineapple. Suppresses inflammation. A main constituent, an antibacterial enzyme called bromelain, is anti-inflammatory. Pineapple aids digestion, helps dissolve blood clots and is good for preventing osteoporosis and bone fractures because of its very high manganese content. It is also antibacterial and antiviral and mildly estrogenic.

-Plum. Antibacterial. Antiviral. Laxative.

-Potato (white). Contains anticancer protease inhibitors. High in potassium, thus may help prevent high blood pressure and strokes. Some estrogenic activity.

-Prune. A well-known laxative. High in fiber, sorbitol and natural aspirin.

-Pumpkin. Extremely high in beta carotene, the antioxidant reputed to help ward off numerous health problems, including heart attacks, cancer, cataracts.

-Raspberry. Antiviral, anticancer activity. High in natural aspirin.

-Rice. Anti-diarrhea, anticancer activity. Like other seeds, contains anticancer protease inhibitors. Of all grains and cereals, it is the least likely to provoke intestinal gas or adverse reactions (intolerances), causing bowel distress such as spastic colon. Rice bran is excellent against constipation, lowers cholesterol and tends to block development of kidney stones.

-Seaweed and Kelp (brown or Laminaria type seaweed). Antibacterial and antiviral activity in brown Laminaria type seaweed known as kelp. It kills herpes virus, for example. Kelp may also lower blood pressure and cholesterol. Wakame boosts immune functioning. Nori kills bacteria and seems to help heal ulcers. A chemical from Wakame seaweed is a clot-buster, in one test twice as powerful as the common drug heparin. Most types of seaweed have anticancer activity. Might aggravate acne flare-ups.

-Soybean. Rich in hormones, it boosts estrogen levels in postmenopausal women. Has anticancer activity and is thought to be especially antagonistic to breast cancer, possibly one reason rates of breast and prostate cancers are low among the Japanese. Soybeans are the richest source of potent protease inhibitors which are anticancer, antiviral agents. Soybeans lower blood cholesterol substantially. In animals, soybeans seem to deter and help dissolve kidney stones.

-Spinach. Tops the list, along with other green leafy vegetables, as a food most eaten by people who don't get cancer. A super source of antioxidants and cancer antagonists, containing about four times more beta carotene and three times more lutein than broccoli, for example. Rich in fiber that helps lower blood cholesterol. Some of its antioxidants are destroyed by cooking. Eat raw or lightly cooked.

-Strawberry. Antiviral, anticancer activity. Often eaten by people less likely to develop all types of cancer.

-Sugar. Helps heal wounds when applied externally. Like other carbohydrates, sugar helps induce cavities. Also may be related to Crohn's disease. Triggers rises in blood sugar and stimulates insulin production.

-Sweet Potato (yams). A source of the antioxidant beta carotene, linked to preventing heart disease, cataracts, strokes and numerous cancers. One half cup of mashed sweet potatoes contains about 14 milligrams of beta carotene, or about 23,000 international units (IUs), according to Department of Agriculture figures.

-Tea (including black, oolong and green tea, not herbal teas). Amazing and diverse pharmacological activity, mainly due to catechins. Tea acts as an anticoagulant, artery protector, antibiotic, anti-ulcer agent, cavity-fighter, anti-diarrhea agent, antiviral agent, diuretic (caffeine), analgesic (caffeine), mild sedative (decaffeinated). In animals tea and tea compounds are potent blockers of various cancers. Tea drinkers appear to have less atherosclerosis (damaged, clogged arteries) and fewer strokes. Excessive tea drinking because of its caffeine could aggravate anxiety, insomnia and symptoms of PMS. Tea may also promote kidney stones because of its high oxalate content. Green tea, popular in Asian countries, is highest in catechins, followed by oolong and ordinary black tea, common in the United States. Green tea is considered most potent. One human study, however, found no difference in benefits to arteries from green or black tea.

-Tomato. A major source of lycopene, an antioxidant and anticancer agent that intervenes in devastating chain reactions of oxygen free radical molecules. Tomatoes are linked in particular to lower rates of pancreatic cancer and cervical cancer.

-Turmeric. Truly one of the marvelous medicinal spices of the world. Its main active ingredient is curcumin which gives turmeric its intense cadmium yellow color. Curcumin, studies show, is an anti-inflammatory agent on a par with cortisone, and has reduced inflammation in animals and symptoms of rheumatoid arthritis in humans. In other tests, it lowered cholesterol, hindered platelet aggregation (blood clotting), protected the liver from toxins, boosted stomach defenses against acid, lowered blood sugar in diabetics, and was a powerful antagonist of numerous cancer-causing agents. Anticancer activity.

-Watermelon. High amounts of lycopene and glutathione, antioxidant and anticancer compounds. Also mild antibacterial, anticoagulant activity.

-Wheat. High-fiber whole wheat, and particularly wheat bran, rank as the world's greatest preventives of constipation. The bran is potently anticancer. Remarkably, in humans, wheat bran can suppress that can develop into colon cancer. Anti-parasitic. Ranks exceedingly high as a trigger of food intolerances and allergies, resulting in symptoms of rheumatoid arthritis, irritable bowel syndrome and neurological illnesses.

-Yogurt. An ancient wonder food, strongly antibacterial and anticancer. A cup or two of yogurt a day boosts immune functioning by stimulating production of gamma interferon. Also spurs activity of natural killer cells that attack viruses and tumors. A daily cup of yogurt reduced colds and other upper respiratory infections in humans. Helps prevent and cure diarrhea. A daily cup of yogurt with acidophilus cultures prevents vaginitis (yeast infections) in women. Helps fight bone problems, such as osteoporosis, because of high available calcium content. Acidophilus yogurt cultures neutralize cancer-causing agents in the intestinal tract. Plain old yogurt with L. bulgaricus and S. thermophilus cultures, both live and dead, blocked lung cancers in animals. Yogurt with live cultures is safe for people with lactose intolerance.

SUPERFOODS

Though there are many nourishing foods, there are only a few superfoods that contain such a potent collection of protective factors that they deserve regular inclusion in most diets.

-Garlic. This stinky little vegetable has been used for 5000 years in various healing formulas. Pasteur noted that garlic killed all of the bacteria in his petri dishes. More importantly, garlic has been found to stimulate natural protection against tumor cells. Tarig Abdullah, MD of Florida found that white blood cells from garlic-fed people were able to kill 139% more tumor cells than white cells from non-garlic eaters.[3] Garlic and onions fed to lab animals helped to decrease the number of skin tumors.[4] Researchers found that onions provided major protection against expected tumors from DMBA in test animals.[5] Mice with a genetic weakness toward cancer were fed raw garlic with a lower-than-expected tumor incidence.[6]

The most common form of cancer worldwide is stomach cancer. Chinese researchers find that a high intake of garlic and onions cuts the risk for stomach cancer in half.[7] Garlic provides the liver with a certain amount of protection against carcinogenic chemicals. Scientists find that garlic is deadly to invading pathogens or tumor cells, but is harmless to normal healthy body cells; thus offering the hope of the truly selective toxin against cancer that is being sought worldwide.

-Carotenoids. Green plants create sugars by capturing the sun's energy in a process called photosynthesis. The electrons that must be corralled in this process can be highly destructive. Hence, nature has evolved an impressive system of free radical protectors, including carotenoids and bioflavonoids, that act like the lead lining in a nuclear reactor to absorb dangerous unpaired electrons. Both of these substances have potential in stimulating the immune system while there is preliminary evidence that carotenoids may be directly toxic to tumor cells.

Carotenoids are found in green and orange fruits and vegetables. Bioflavonoids are found in citrus, whole grains, honey, and other plant foods.

-*Cruciferous vegetables*. Broccoli, Brussels sprout, cabbage, and cauliflower were involved in the "ground floor" discovery that nutrition is linked to cancer. Lee Wattenberg, MD of the University of Minnesota found in the 1970s that animals fed cruciferous vegetables had markedly lower cancer rates than matched controls. Since then, the active ingredient "indoles" have been isolated from cruciferous vegetables and found to be very protective against cancer. Scientists at Johns Hopkins University found that lab animals fed cruciferous vegetables and then exposed to  the deadly carcinogen aflatoxin had a 90 percent reduction in their cancer rate.[8]

Cruciferous vegetables are able to increase the body's production of glutathione peroxidase, which is one of the more important protective enzyme systems in the body.

-*Mushrooms*. Gourmet chefs have long prized various mushrooms for their subtle and exotic flavors. Now there is an abundance of scientific evidence showing that Rei-shi, Shiitake, and Maitake mushrooms are potent anti-cancer foods.[9] Actually, Maitake literally means "dancing mushroom" since people would dance with joy when finding these delicate mushrooms on a country hillside. Oral extract of Maitake provided complete elimination of tumors in 40% of animals tested, while the remaining 60% of animals had a 90% elimination of tumors. Maitake contains a polysaccharide, called beta-glucan, which stimulates the immune system and even lowers blood pressure.

-*Legumes*. Seed foods (like soybeans) have a substance that can partially protect the seed from digestion, called protease inhibitors (PI). For many years, these substances were thought to be harmful. New evidence finds that PIs may squelch tumor growth.[10] Researchers at the National Cancer Institute find a collection of substances in soybeans, including isoflavones and phytoestrogens, appear to have potent anti-cancer properties.[11] Dr. Ann Kennedy has spent 20 years researching a compound in soybeans that:

-prevents cancer in most animals exposed to a variety of carcinogens

-retards cancer in some studies

-lowers the toxic side effects of chemo and radiation therapy

-reverts a cancer cell back to a normal healthy cell.[12]

-Others. There are numerous foods that show an ability to slow tumor growth in some way. Apples, apricots, barley, citrus fruit, cranberries, fiber, figs, fish oil, fish, ginger, green tea, spinach, seaweed and other foods are among the reasons that I heavily favor the use of a mixed highly nutritious diet as the foundation for nutrition in cancer therapy.

Food treats malnutrition. Food contains known essential nutrients that stimulate the immune system and provide valuable protection against carcinogens. Foods also contain poorly understood factors that may add measurably to the recovery of the cancer patient. Many foods have tremendous therapeutic value in helping the patient to internally fight cancer.

-*Yogurt*. While dairy products are the world's most common allergenic food, for 1/2 to 2/3 of the population, yogurt can provide some dramatic immune stimulation. On the surface, yogurt appears to be nothing more than a fermented dairy product. Yet, modern scientists find that the active culture of bacteria in yogurt (Lactobacillus) can fortify the immune system. Yogurt is an impressive immune stimulant.[13] In both humans and animals, yogurt in the diet tripled the internal production of interferon (a powerful weapon of the immune system against tumor cells) while also raising the level of natural killer cells. Yogurt has been shown to slow down the growth of tumor cells in the GI tract while improving the ability of the immune system to destroy active tumor cells.[14] Yogurt can block the production of carcinogenic agents in the colon. When scientists looked at the diet of 1010 women with breast cancer and compared them to an equally matched group without breast cancer, they found an inverse dose-dependent relationship: the more yogurt consumed, the lower the risk for breast cancer.[15]

In several European studies, yogurt in animal studies was able to reverse tumor progress. A 1962 study found that 59 percent of 258 mice implanted with sarcoma cells were cured through yogurt. A more recent American study found a 30 percent cure rate through yogurt.[16] While it is doubtful that yogurt is going to cure advanced human cancer, it is likely that yogurt can better fortify the cancer patient's immune system.

PATIENT PROFILE: SURVIVING KIDNEY CANCER
M.M. was diagnosed with renal cell carcinoma stage 4. She took thalidomide and interferon for nearly 2 years, then stopped these medications due to side effects, which included vomiting, headaches, and neuropathy (numb and painful hands and feet). M.M. used the nutrition guidelines in this book along with mistletoe and dendritic cell therapy to shrink her tumor by 30%. She was given 6 months to live, yet has survived 5 years, although she still has tumor burden. Her quality of life is good. M.M. says that "we are all terminal. Just try to make a difference in someone else's life."

ENDNOTES

[1] . Stahl, W. and Sies, H. lycopene: a biologically important carotenoid for humans? Arch. Biochem. Biophys. 336: 1-9, 1996

[2] . Gerster, H. The potential role of lycopene for human health. J. Amer. Coll. Nutr. 16: 109-126, 1997

[3] . Abdullah, TH, et al., *Journal of the National Medical Association*, vol.80, no.4, p.439, Apr.1988

[4] . Belman, S., *Carcinogenesis*, vol.4, no.8, p.1063, 1983

[5] . Kiukian, K., et al., *Nutrition and Cancer*, vol.9, p.171, 1987

[6] . Kroning, F., *Acta Unio Intern. Contra. Cancrum, vol.20, no.3, p.855, 1964*

[7] . You, WC, et al., *Journal of the National Cancer Institute*, vol.81, p.162, Jan.18, 1989

[8] . Ansher, SS, *Federation of Chemistry and Toxicology*, vol.24, p.405, 1986

[9] . Chihara, G., et al., Cancer Detection and Prevention, vol.1, p.423, 1987 suppl.

[10] . Kennedy, A., and Little, JB, *Cancer Research*, vol.41, p.2103, 1981

[11] . Messina, M., et al., Journal National Cancer Institute, vol.83, no.8, p.541, Apr.1991

[12] . Oreffo, VI, et al., Toxicology, vol.69, no.2, p.165, 1991; see also von Hofe, E, et al., Carcinogenesis, vol.12, no.11, p.2147, Nov.1991; see also Su, LN, et al., Biochemical & Biophysical Research Communications, vol.176, no.1, p.18, Apr.1991

[13] . Conge, G., et al., *Reproduction, Nutrition, Development* (French), vol. 20, p.929, 1980

[14] . Hitchins, AD, and McDonough, FE, *American Journal of Clinical Nutrition*, vol.49, p.675, 1989

[15] . Le, MG, et al., *Journal of the National Cancer Institute*, vol.77, p.633, 1986

[16] . Shahani, KM, et al., *Society of Applied Bacteriology Symposium Serial, vol.11, p.257, 1983*

CHAPTER 6
WHAT'S IN A
WHOLE FRESH APPLE?
THE FOOD, THE WHOLE FOOD AND
NOTHING BUT THE FOOD

"Let food be your medicine and medicine be your food."
Hippocrates, father of modern medicine, 400 B.C

FROM NATURE'S PHARMACY: PECTIN. When the nutritionists of the early 20th century found that a large part of plant food is indigestible fiber, they reasoned: "Since you cannot digest or absorb this stuff, then it must be useless, or even counterproductive." We now find that the value in fiber is its indigestible nature. Soluble fibers include pectin, and are extremely useful both in the human gut for health and in the food industry because pectin binds water and makes a gel like consistency in  foods like jam and jelly. Pectin has been shown to reduce serum cholesterol while also feeding the friendly bacteria that help to produce vitamins (like biotin and K) and compete with the unfriendly bacteria and fungus that can turn our large intestines into a war zone. Nobel prize winner Ilya Metchnikov in 1908 began the field of probiotics and prebiotics with his declaration "death begins in the colon." 40% of the body's immune system surrounds the colon. The health of our gut is crucial to our overall health. Pectin becomes a magical "broom" sweeping out the intestines of debris and pathogens before they can do any damage. With the generous amount of pectin in apples, maybe the old expression "an apple a day keeps the doctor away" has some merit. Pectin from citrus peelings has been processed to create "modified" citrus pectin, which has shown some activity against various forms of human cancer.

We are only beginning to fully appreciate the elegant symphony of nutrients available in whole foods. To naively and arrogantly believe that we can tamper with this time-tested formula and improve on it is just plain foolish. Just to give you a sampling of the incredible array of substances found in whole food, let's look at a chemical analysis of what is found in whole fresh unsprayed apples. You have heard that expression,"An apple a day keeps the doctor away." Maybe its true. The list below helps you to appreciate the complexity of whole foods. To continue your pursuit of phytochemicals, go to the taxpayer supported National Library of Medicine website where 11 million scientific studies have been read and cataloged. The volume of information is dazzling. **http://www.ncbi.nlm.nih.gov/sites/entrez:**

WHAT'S IN A FRESH WHOLE CLEAN APPLE?

from "Handbook of Phytochemical Constituents of Generally Regarded as Safe (GRAS) Herbs" and Hulme acta agric scand suppl 22:1980

abscisic-acid fr nap	ash 2,300-43,000 fr aas usg
cis-2, trans-4-abscisic-acid bk nap	asparagine 171 fr
trans-abscisic-acid fr nap	aspartic-acid 210-2,115 fr usa
acetic-acid	avicularin fr nap
acetic-acid-amyl-ester	barium 0.22-8.6 fr usg
acetaldehyde	benzoic-acid
acetone	3,4-benzopyrene fr nap
n-alpha-acetyl-agginine sh nap	benzyl-acetate
adenine rt nap	benzyl-amine 0.6 ep(fr) nap
alpha-alanine fr	benzylamine 0.3-3.0 fr nap
beta-alanine fr	biotin
alanine 70-435 fr usa	boron 1-110 fr aas bob usg
aluminum 0.4-129 fr aas usg	bromine <1 fr aas
alpha-aminobutyric-acid	butanol
ammonia (NH3) 235-1,029 EP(FR)	n-butanol
amygdalin 6,000-13,800 sd	1-butanol
amyl-acetate	2-butanol
amyl-butyrate	butyl-acetate
amyl-propionate	butyl-butyrate
aniline 1.7 ep(fr) nap	butyl-caproate
aniline 1.5 fr nap	butyl-propionate
arabinose	butyl-valerianate
arginine 60-373 fr usa	i-butyl-octanoate
arsenic 0.00055-0.43 fr aas usg	i-butyl-propioante
ascorbic-acid 20-402 fr usa	n-butyl-decanoate
ascorbidase	n-butyl-formate

n-butyl-n-hexanoate
n-butyl-octanoate
n-butyl-propionate
cadmium <0.002-0.0258 fr aas usg
caffeetannin
caffeic-acid 85-1,270 fr crc(fsn)
calcium 43-750 (-1,376) fr aas usg
calcium-oxalate
caproaldehyde
caproic-acid-amyl-ester
caprylic-ester
carobohydrate 152,250-948,550 fr
beta-carotene 0-76 fr
carotenoids 0-126
catalase
d-catechin fr nap
chlorogenic-acid fr nap
chlorophyll 0-1 fr
chromium 0.005-0.3 fr aas usg
citric-acid
citramalic-acid
cobalt <0.005-0.043 fr aas usg
copper 0.24-4 fr aas usg
coumaric-acid
p-coumaric-acid 15-460 fr crc(fsn)
n-coumaryl-quinic-acid
p-coumaryl-quinic-acid fr nap
creatine sh nap
cutin ep(fr) nap
cyanidin lf nap
cyanidin-3-arabinoside
cyanidin-7-arabinoside
cynanidin-3,5-diglucoside cy nap
cyanidin-3-galactoside
cystine 30-187
i-decanoic-acid
n-decanol
decenoic-acid
i-decyl-acetate
dehydroascorbic-acid
diastase
diethylamine 3 fr nap
digalactosyl-diglyceride 49-107 fr
3-beta-19-alpha-dihydroxy-2-oxo-urs-
12-en-28-oic-acid 1,000 wd nap
dihydroxytricarballylic-acid 1 fr
diphosphatidyl-glycerol 4-6 fr
eo 25-35 fr
l-epicatechin fr nap

5,6-epoxy-10'-apo-5,6-dihydro-beta-
carotene-3,10'-diol 20,000 ep(fr) nap
estragole tr eo
estrone 0.10-0.13 sd nap
ethanol
ethyl-acetate
ethylamine 3 fr nap
ethyl-butyrate
ethyl-caproate
ethyl-crotonate
ethyl-decenoate
ethyl-dodecanoate
ethyl-hexanoate
ethyl-isobutyrate
ethyl-methylbutyrate
ethyl-nonanoate
ethyl-octanoate
ethyl-pentanoate
ethyl-phenacetate
ethyl-propionate
ethyl-valerianate
farnesene ep(fr) nap
fat 3,210-34,200 fr fnf ped
fat 180,00-230,000 sd
ferulic-acid 4-95 fr crc(fsn)
fiber 131,000 fr ped
fiber 5,200-49,636 fr usa
fluorine <0.1-2.1 fr aas
folacin 0.02-0.2 fr usa
formic-acid
fructose 50,100-60,800 fr
fumaric-acid
galactanase
galactaric-acid
d-galacturonic-acid 13-54
geraniol
d-glucitol
glucocerebroside 34-49
d-gluconic-acid
glucose 17,200-18,200 fr
glutamic-acid 156-1,244 fr
glutamine 20
glyceric-acid
glycine 80-497
glycolic-acid
glyoxylic-acid
guanidine sh nap
guanidinoacetic-acid sh nap
gamma-guanidinobutramide sh nap

gamma-guanidinobutyric-acid sh nap
gamma-guanidinopropionic-acid sh
guanidinosuccinic-acid sh nap
hemicellulose
heptacosane
n-heptanoic-acid
heptenoic-acid
2-heptanol
n-heptanol
n-hex-1-en-3-ol
cis-n-hex-3-en-1-ol
trans-n-hex-2-en-1-ol
trans-n-hex-3-en-1-ol
hexacosanol
n-hexanol
7-hexanoic-acid
i-hexanoic-acid
hexanol
2-hexenal
trans-2-hexenoic-acid
hexyl-acetate
hexyl-butyrate
hexyl-formate
n-hehyl-n-hexanoate
n-hexyl-octanoate
n-hexyl-propionate
histidine 30-187 fr
p-hydroxybenzoic-acid fr nap
hydroxycinnamic-acid 1,340 fr
4-hydroxymethylproline
3-hydroxy-octyl-beta-d-glucoside fr
19-hydroxyursolic-acid pl jsg
20-hydroxyursolic-acid pl jsg
19-hydroxyursonic-acid pl jsg
hyperin
hyperoside fr nap
idaein
indole-3-acetic-acid pl pas
inositol
iodine
iron 1.1-123 fr aas usa usg
isoamyl-butyrate
isoamyl-propionate
isobutyl-acetate
isobutyl-butyrate
isobutyl-formate
isochlorogenic-acid pl pas
isocitric-acid
isoleucine 50-497 fr

isopropyl-butyrate
isoquercitrin fr nap
jasmonic-acid fr nap
kilocalories 3,419 fr ped
lactic-acid
lauric-acid 10-63 fr
lead 0.002-64 fr aas usg
lecithin
leucine 120-746 fr
linolenic-acid 870-5,411 fr omega-3
alpha-linolenic-acid 180-1,120 fr
omega-3
lithium 0.044-0.172 fr usg
lutein 0.4-5 fr jaf37:657
luteoxanthin fr nap
lysine 20-746 fr
magnesium 48-478 (-860) fr aas usa
usg
l-malic-acid
malvidin-monoglycoside
manganese 0-29 fr aas usg
mannose
mercury 0.00011-0.02 fr aas usg
methanol
methionine 20-124
methyl-acetate
methyl-2-xi-acetoxy-20-beta-hydroxy-
ursonate ep(fr)
methylamine 4.5 ep(fr) nap
2-methyl-but-2-en-1-al fr nap
2-methyl-but-3-en-1-ol fr nap
d-2-methylbutan-1-ol
2-methylbutan-2-ol
methyl-butyrate
methyl-caproate
2-methyl-2,3-epoxy-pentane fr nap
24-methylene-cholesterol po nap
methyl-formate
methyl-guanidine sh nap
6-methyl-hepten-5-en-2-one fr nap
methyl-hexanoate
n-methyl-beta-phenethylamine 1.2 fr
nap
methyl-propionate
methyl-2-methyl-butyrate
methyl-i-pentanoate
methyl-n-pentanoate
2-methylpentan-2-ol

n-methyl-phenethylamine   1.3   ex(fr) nap
n-methyl-phenethylamine 1.2 fr nap
gamma-methyl-proline
2-methyl-propen-1-al fr nap
methyl-vinyl-ketone fr nap
mevalonic-acid 30-36 fr
molybdenum 0.077-0.43 fr usg
monogalactosyl-diglyceride 12-42
1-mono-linolein sd nap
mufa 150-935 fr usa
myoinositol 4,500 po nap
myristic-acid 20-124 fr
neochlorogenic-acid
neoxanthin ep(fr) nap
niacin 1-7 fr
nickel 0.004-0.645 fr aas usg
nitrogen 280-4,000 fr aas
nonacosane
d-l-nonacosanol
n-nonanoic-acid
n-nonanol-2-nonanol
nonenoic-acid
1-nonyl-acetate
octacosanol
octa-cis-3-cis-5-dien-1-ol eo nap
octa-trans-3-cis-5-dien-1-ol eo nap
octa-cis-3-cis-5-dien-1-ol-acetate eo
octa-trans-3-cis-5-dien-1-ol-acetate
n-octanone
n-octanol-2-octanol
octenoic-acid
1-octyl-acetate
oleic-acid 140-871 fr
oxalic-acid
oxaloacetic-acid
alpha-oxoglutaric-acid
palmitic-acid 480-2,986 fr
palmitoleic-acid 10-62 fr
pantothenic-acid 1-4 fr usa
pectase
pectin 1,400-66,585 fr usa
pectin-demethoxyxylase
n-pentanoic-acid
i-pentanoic-acid
pentanol
i-pentanol
2-pentanol
3-pentanol

n-pentenoic-acid
n-pentyl-amine 0.3 fr nap
pentyl-butyrate
n-pentyl-decanoate
n-pentyl-formate
i-pentyl-formate
pentyl-hexanoate
n-pentyl-2-methylbutyrate
i-pentyl-i-pentanoate
n-pentyl-octanoate
peroxidase
2-phenethylacetate
phenolics 1,100-3,400
phenylalanine 50-311 fr
phloretamide fr nap
phloretin lf jad
phloretin-4'-o-beta-d-glucopyranoside
6,486 fr nap
phloretin-xyloglucoside fr nap
phlorizin
phosphatidylic-acid 3-6 fr
phosphatidyl-choline 189-214 fr
phosphatidyl-ethanolamine 101-124 fr
phosphatidyl-glycerol 8-27 fr
phosphatidyl-inositol 53-59 fr
phosphatidyl-serine 4 fr
phosphorus 68-925 (-1,548) fr aas
phytosterols 120-745 fr usa
pipecolinic-acid
polygalactosyl-diglyceride
polygalacturonase
polyphenolase
pomolic-acid pl jsg
pomonic-acid pl jsg
potassium 1,110-12,140 (-17,630) fr
procyanidins lf nap
proline 20-435
propanol
2-propanol
n-propanol
i-propanol
n-propionic-acid
propyl-acetate
propyl-butyrate
propyl-formate
propyl-2-methylbutyrate
propyl-n-pentanoate
propyl-propionate
protein 1,870-12,800 fr ped

protocatechuic-acid fr nap
pufa 1,050-6,535 fr usa
pyrrolidine 1.5 ep(fr) nap
pyroxidine
pyruvic-acid
quercetin 58-263 pc pam
quercetin-arabinoside
quercetin-3-o-alpha-
arabinofuranoside pl jsg
quercetin-3-o-alpha-galactoside ep(fr)
quercetin-3-o-beta-d-glucoside pl jsg
quercetin-3-rhamnoglucoside
quercetin-3-o-rhamnoside pl jsg
quercetin-3-rutinoside
quercetin-3-o-xyloside ep(fr) nap
quercitrin fr nap
l-quinic-acid
reynoutrin fr nap
riboflavin 1 fr
rubidium 0.27-10 fr aas
rutin tr ep(fr) nap
selenium 0.000055-0.00043 fr usg
serline 80-497 fr usa
sfa 580-3,610 fr usa
shikimic-acid
silicon 1-70 fr aas
silver 0.011-0.086 fr usg
sinapic-acid fr nap
sodium 0-133 fr usg

sorbitol lf nap
stearic-acid 70-435 fr
strontium 0.165-8.6 fr usg
succinic-acid
sucrose 24,000-36,200 fr
sugar 60,100-166,000 fr
sulfur 1.65-23 fr usg
tetradecenyl-acetate lf nap
tetradecyl-acetate lf nap
thiamin 1-2 fr ped
threonine 30-435 fr
titanium 0.055-3 fr usg
alpha-tocopherol 2-37 fr tot usa
triacontanol
triglyceride 45-50
1,3,3,-trimethyl-dioxa-2,7-
bicyclo(2,2,1)heptane fr nap
tryptophan 20-124 fr
tyrosine 40-249 fr
uronic-acid 7-1,440 fr
ursolic-acid ep(fr) nap
valine 40-560 fr
vit-b6 1-3 fr
vomifoliol-1-o-beta-d-xylopyranosyl-6-
o-beta-d-glucopyranoside fr nap
water 809,000-896,000 fr usg
xylose
zinc 0-35 fr aas usg
zirconium 0.22-0.86 fr usg

PATIENT PROFILE: S.J. was a 45 year old brilliant tax attorney, trained at the finest schools, whose successful career was jeopardized when he started losing his memory in front of audiences. The finest medical center on the west coast did a complete battery of neurological examinations on S.J., recommending a new experimental drug. S.J. took the list of side effects from this new drug to his physician who did a patient history on S.J. Turns out, S.J. was a "junkie" for diet soft drinks, containing aspartame, which is a neurological poison.[1] S.J.'s doctor suggested going without the usual 3-6 diet soft drinks daily. S.J. had nothing to lose in avoiding diet soft drink. His memory returned fully within 2 weeks.

[1] . Blaylock, R., EXCITOTOXINS, Health Press, 1996

CHAPTER 7
NUTRITITOUS AND DELICIOUS
MEAL PLAN AND RECIPES

"Behold, I have given you every green plant, and it shall be food for you."   *Genesis 1:29*

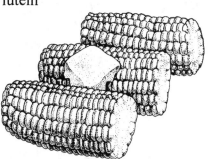

FROM NATURE'S PHARMACY: lutein
Macular degeneration is a blindness that affects 1.2 million Americans, mostly over age 65. There is a growing body of data showing that lutein and its cousin carotenoid xeaxanthin may be able to prevent or delay the onset of macular degeneration. Lutein is an orange colored substance found mostly in green vegetables and used by plants as part of photosynthesis. In the human eye, lutein is used as a "buffer" or antioxidant to reduce the damage from blue light on the "screen" of the eye, the retina. Best sources of lutein include leafy greens (like spinach, kale, collards), broccoli, zucchini, peas, corn, brussel sprouts. Most Americans do not get enough lutein.

THE IMPORTANCE OF A GOOD DIET
Eating is essential for life. Yet eating should also be a celebration of life. Note how often people center their celebrations (wedding, birthday, anniversary, holidays) around food. This is all wonderful. Yet, modern humans are among the first group in history to have more food than we need and an amazing variety of tempting treats at the grocery store. Poor food choices and excessive food intake have led to many diseases of civilization. This chapter is not a

cook book. There are plenty of cook books at your local bookstore. This chapter offers some ideas for meal plans and a few recipe ideas. As you begin to make better choices in the grocery store, in your kitchen while preparing foods, and at the dinner table; you should note some improvements in your physical and mental energy levels. May you find foods that are both nutritious to nourish your body and delicious to nourish your appetite.

TO JUSTIFY THE PURCHASE OF A QUALITY BLENDER

1) TEETH. If you know that fruits, vegetables, nuts, whole grains, and legumes are good for you, but you don't have the teeth chewing power, then puree or grind up these wholesome foods and eat them. I puree almonds and pecans and put a large spoon of this nut meal in my oatmeal for breakfast. Delicious.

2) NEAR FREE RICE MILK. If you buy rice milk, then start making your own. Soak ½ cup of brown rice in 5 cups of water overnight in your pressure cooker. Next day, cook the mixture, allowing the pressure cooker to rock for 4 minutes. Let cool. Puree this rice mixture with ½ teaspoon of salt, 2 tablespoons of olive oil, and 1 heaping tablespoon of thick unpasteurized honey. Makes 5 cups. Delightful!

3) KID FOOD. If you can't get the kids to eat their fruits and vegetables, then puree it for them to drink. Take 100% frozen grape juice concentrate, add water according to directions into a pitcher. Take ½ cup of peeled and cut up carrots, 1 cup of grape juice from above, blend on high. Add ½ banana then blend again. A rich smooth tasting cornucopia of Nature's finest phytochemicals for health.

4) 5 TO STAY ALIVE. The National Institutes of Health have recommended that everyone eat 5 servings daily of fruits and vegetables. More would be even better. But the most commonly eaten vegetables in America are, in order: catsup, french fries, and onion rings. I am not kidding. None of these vegetables have the nutritional merits of real produce. You can puree almost any fruit or vegetable in your high speed blender and make it possible to meet this crucial health guideline of "five to stay alive".

5) MYSTERY "SOUPE DU JOUR" (French for "soup of the day"). You have leftovers in your refrigerator and everyone is hungry. Take the leftovers: to the vegetables (including cooked potatoes) add some fluid; such as rice milk (see above) or milk, or chicken or beef broth, then puree all in your blender, add seasonings (like soy sauce, curry, miso, see chart for "healthier seasonings"), warm on stove. To this soup, add some cut up turkey, chicken, pork, beef, fish.

6) WEIGHT LOSS. On a whole food diet, it is difficult to gain weight. On a standard processed food diet, it is difficult to lose weight. Start eating more plant food (grains, legumes, fruits, vegetables, nuts) with the fiber and fluid intact. You will find yourself fuller sooner at meal time. Weight loss becomes nearly effortless when you eat the right foods.

7) REGULARITY. A daily bowel movement is an unfulfilled dream for many constipated Americans. By eating more wholesome plant food with your blender, you will be getting more fiber to increase stool bulk which provides for a healthy daily bowel movement. At least two food empires, Kellogg cereals and Graham crackers, were founded on the principle that a little fiber works wonders in promoting daily bowel movements, which has major repercussions in overall health. Surgeons have told me that bowel obstructions in colon cancer is an ugly way to go. Many Americans are living in a chronic state of bowel obstructions via constipation via not enough fiber in the diet. Get unplugged. Get regular.

8) CHEAP HEALTH INSURANCE. Most Americans now pay, either personally or through their employer, $1000 per person per month for health insurance. As mentioned in the chapter on "health meltdown", much of that money is spent on conditions that are usually preventable, including diabetes, heart disease, hypertension, and cancer. There was a commercial selling regular oil changes for your car that stated: "You can pay me now or you can pay me later." That statement is even more true with preventive health steps than it is with your car. Over 200 scientific studies show that a diet rich in wholesome fruits and vegetables lowers the risk for cancer, heart disease, diabetes, obesity, and more. Since the most commonly eaten vegetables in America are (I am not kidding): catsup, french fries, and onion rings; you probably do not eat enough fruits and vegetables in your diet.

9) TRULY GOLDEN YEARS. We often refer to our retirement years as the "golden years", and they can be. But for too many Americans, the golden years are spent waiting in a doctor's office for the test results, or recovering from surgery. Various surveys have found that Americans are not as concerned with death as they are with incapacitation, specifically Alzheimer's and blindness. Eating more fruits and vegetables provides numerous nutrients that will help prevent these above ugly diseases of later life. Would you rather be hiking or hurting? Golfing or grumbling? The envy of the cruise ship, or staying home?

10) MAKE YOUR OWN FLOUR. Seeds, like flax, wheat, rice or oats, can last years when kept in a cool place. Once you grind the seeds, the clock for deterioration of the food begins. Whole oat flour has one tenth the shelf life of oat seeds. Buy the seeds, then make the flour in your blender as you need it. Saves money. Gives you a nice inventory of storage food. Keeps your food fresh.

11) MEAL REPLACEMENT. Ever have someone in your home who could not or would not eat? Sick child? Cancer patient? Ever have someone who has to dash out the door early in the morning with a cup of coffee and pastry in hand, knowing that is not a good breakfast, but it seems like there isn't enough time to prepare and eat a good breakfast before leaving in the morning? Use your high speed blender to create the following fabulous meal replacement that takes only a few minutes to prepare and can be consumed in the car en route to school, work, or the airport.

DRAGON-SLAYER SHAKE

While most of us are familiar with milkshakes, there are many variations on that theme that can provide nutrient-dense foods in a convenient format. Shakes can be a quick and easy breakfast. Depending on your calorie requirements, use this shake in addition to or instead of the breakfast suggestions listed later.

You can take your vitamin or drug pills with the "Dragon-Slayer. The creamy texture of this "shake" helps the pills go down the esophagus more smoothly. Notice the general combination of ingredients. Get creative with this general guideline. Many a cancer patient has told me that this "dragon slayer" shake has saved their life when they could not or would not eat a decent meal.

DRAGONSLAYER SHAKE: general combination of ingredients				
liquid 4-8 oz	protein1-4 T	vegetables	thicken 2T	other 1-3 T.
water fruit juice vegetable j. V8 ice cubes milk soy milk rice milk	egg,soy, rice powder beef whey bee pollen dry milk wheat germ flax meal spirulina brewer yeast	raw or cook carrots, beets broccoli cauliflower cabbage tomto,onion asparagus spinach, kale collards	froze banana apple sauce agar carragenan guar gum gelatin ice cubes	MCT lecithin powdr greens aloe Perfect 7 vit/min powd ImmunoPw flax oil

Ingredients:
- ➤ 4-8 ounces of liquid
- ➤ 10-15 grams (1-4 tablespoons) of powdered protein
- ➤ 1/4 to 1/2 cup vegetables, cooked or raw
- ➤ 1-3 tablespoons thickening agent
- ➤ 1-3 tablespoons of other ingredients, including ImmunoPower (GettingHealthier.com), Perfect 7, flax or fish oil.

Banana adds texture via pectin to make this shake have true milk shake viscosity. If the banana is frozen, it will give a thick "milkshake-like" texture to your drink.

For those who need to gain weight, add 2 tablespoons of MCT (medium chain triglyceride) oil from your health food store.

Directions:
Using a powerful blender puree all ingredients.

ONE WEEK OF NUTRITIOUS AND DELICIOUS EATING
MONDAY
Breakfast:
instant pudding with yogurt in pita bread, fruit in season
Lunch:
chicken sandwich with fruit salad
Dinner:
Baked or broiled salmon with herbs, fast vegetable soup, evening oats, chocolate cake

TUESDAY
Breakfast
whole wheat English muffin, sesame spread, fruit
Lunch
linguini, cabbage salad
Dinner
Baked chicken, yams, California spinach salad, frozen yogurt pie

WEDNESDAY
Breakfast
Dragon Slayer drink, toast
Lunch
pita bread sandwich, onion soup
Dinner
Turkey loaf, homemade applesauce, sprout salad with peaches and almonds, pita bread, miso dessert balls

THURSDAY
Breakfast
Apple bran muffin, yogurt
Lunch
Cottage cheese sandwich, fresh piece of fruit
Dinner
Pressure cooked stew, rye bread, carob cookies

FRIDAY
Breakfast
Shredded wheat cereal with apple juice, yogurt and fruit
Lunch

turkey bacon, tomato and onion sandwich, spinach bean sprout salad
Dinner
crab dinner, fruited rice pilaf, cold Italian veggies, banana pudding.

SATURDAY
Breakfast
Mexican omelette, fruit
Lunch
tofu steak, fruit, tomato juice
Dinner
Turkey sausage pizza, banana waldorf, Chinese chews

SUNDAY
Breakfast
eggs fried in pam or a bit of butter, Anner's blender pancakes, fruit
Lunch
humus in pita bread, candy carrots with nuts
Dinner
turkey, seasoned bulger, orange and onion salad, yogurt pudding

RECIPES FOR THE WEEK
Monday
Yogurt Pudding
Use 1 box of instant pudding with 2 cups of yogurt. Stir until well
blended. Refrigerate.

Chicken Salad Sandwich
Finely diced chicken
plain yogurt
pickle relish
chopped red or spring onion to taste
salt and pepper (optional)
diced celery (optional)
Spike to taste.

Mix chicken, relish, onion, celery and Spike. Add enough
yogurt to make it the consistency you enjoy. Spread on whole wheat
bread.

Fruit Salad

Any fruit is season chopped into bite size pieces and pour vanilla yogurt over the top.

Baked Salmon

1 whole salmon or piece about 2 1/2 pounds
1/2 cup chopped fresh parsley
2 tablespoons combination of chopped fresh herbs: dill, chives, chervil, basil, sage
1 teaspoon Spike (optional)
1 tablespoon water
1 tablespoon lemon juice

Place salmon on foil. Sprinkle herbs to taste inside cavity. Mix water with lemon juice and sprinkle over outside of salmon. Fold foil over and seal.

Place wrapped salmon on baking sheet and bake in 450 degree oven for 10 minutes for every 1 inch thickness of fish, plus an additional 10 minutes cooking time because it's wrapped in foil (35 to 40 minutes total cooking time), or until salmon is opaque. Unwrap and discard skin; most of it should stick to foil. Place salmon on warmed platter. Garnish with parsley, dill, or watercress if you'd like.

Fast Vegetable Soup

2 cups skim milk (or a milk substitute from soy or rice)
1 tablespoon butter or "better butter"
2 tablespoon whole wheat flour
2 teaspoons Gayelord's all natural vegetable broth
1 teaspoon Spike
1/4 teaspoon pepper (optional)
2 cups cooked vegetables

Put all ingredients in blender in order listed. Cover and blend until smooth. Pour into a saucepan. Cook, stirring occasionally, over low heat until hot.

Evening Oats

1 small to medium apple chopped
1 tbs. butter
1 1/2 cup uncooked oats
1 egg beaten

1/2 cup water
1-2 tbs. honey
1 tsp. cinnamon
1/4 tsp. salt
1/2 tsp vanilla

Saute the apple bits in butter in a skillet. Combine oats and egg in a bowl. Mix. Add oats to apples. Cook over medium heat 3 to 5 minutes, stirring until oats are dry and lightly brown. Add remaining ingredients. Continue cooking, stirring occasionally until liquid evaporates-about 3 minutes. Makes 2 cups.

Chocolate Cake

Whole Wheat Cake bottom:
1/3 cup honey
1/4 cup butter softened
1 egg
2/3 cup yogurt
1-2 tsp. vanilla
1/2 tsp. almond extract (optional)
1 cup whole wheat flour
1 1/2 tsp. baking powder
14 tsp. salt

Cream together honey and butter; add egg, yogurt, and vanilla. Stir. Add remaining ingredients stirring until smooth. Pour batter into greased 8 or 9 inch round baking dish. Bake in oven for 20-25 minutes at 350 F. Let stand, covered, 10 minutes. Store covered until cool.

Chocolate Frosting
1/4 cup butter softened
1/4 cup honey
1-2 teaspoon vanilla
1/2 cup yogurt
3 tablespoons cocoa powder
3 tablespoons carob powder (or a total of 6 tablespoons cocoa powder if you don't want to use carob)
dash of salt (optional)
1/4 cup chopped nuts (optional)
About 1 1/2 cups dry non-fat milk powder (or whey milk substitute)

dry pectin or powdered sugar (optional) for thickener

Mix first 4 ingredients until smooth. Stir in cocoa and carob. Sift or stir in the powder milk. Will be slightly lumpy if just stirred. Mix until slightly runny. Taste to see if mixture needs to be sweeter. Can add powder sugar. The frosting tends to thicken up, so wait a few minutes before frosting the cake for the right consistency. Sprinkle with nuts. Keep in refrigerator. Frosts 2 single layer cakes.

Tuesday

Sesame Spread
3/4 cup sesame seeds
1 tablespoon honey
1/4 cup apple juice or water
1/8 teaspoon salt

Toast sesame seeds and grind into a meal in a blender. Remove to a bowl and add honey, water, and salt. The mixture will thicken as it cools, so you may want to thin it by adding more juice.

Linguini
1/2 pound linguini
1 tablespoon olive oil
1 clove garlic, minced
1/2 cup finely diced mushrooms
1/3 cup minced fresh parsley
1/4 cup grated soy cheese
Lite Salt or salt substitute to taste

Bring 2 quarts of water to a boil in a medium size saucepan. Add the noodles and cook for about 5 minutes. Drain thoroughly. Immediately return the pot to the stove and add the olive oil, garlic, and mushrooms. Cook for 3 minutes over medium heat. Add the drained noodles and parsley, and toss. Add the cheese and salt to taste and toss again.

Cabbage Salad
1/4 of a head of a medium cabbage
2 carrots
1 diced onion (small)
raisins

sunflower seeds
Italian dressing

Grate cabbage and carrots. Add onion, raisins and sunflower seeds to taste. Sprinkle with Italian dressing.

Variation: Add any of the following: diced prunes, diced apples, walnuts, pecans, bell peppers, any other vegetables or dried fruit.

Baked Chicken and Yams

4 pieces of chicken
4 baking yams (medium size)

Wash chicken and place in oven-proof pan with enough room so the pieces aren't crowded. Scrub yams and poke with a knife several times. Place chicken and yams in oven and cook at 375 F. for 45 to 50 minutes.

California Spinach Salad

4 cups torn spinach leaves
1-2 cups alfalfa sprouts
1/4 pound mushrooms, sliced
1 large tomato, cut in chunks
2 spring onions, chopped

Toss ingredients together. Serve with Avocado dressing or your favorite.

Avocado Dressing

1/2 large ripe avocado
1 tablespoon lemon juice
1/8 teaspoon salt
1/8 teaspoon chili powder
squeezed garlic
1/4 cup buttermilk (or milk substitute)

Mix all ingredients well. Serve over salad.

Frozen Yogurt Pie

4 cups of your favorite flavor of frozen yogurt (we like Yarnell's)
8 ounces of Cool whip
9 inch baked whole wheat pie crust

Thaw Cool whip for 4 hours in the refrigerator. Thaw the frozen yogurt just to where you can stir in cool whip. Don't let it get too soft. Place mixture into the pie crust. Freeze.

Wednesday

Pita Bread Sandwich

You can create your own with: cheese, tomato, sprouts, garbanzo beans, grated carrot, sunfower seeds with Italian dressing

Onion Soup

1/2 to 1 tablespoon canola or sesame oil
2 lb. onions, thinly sliced
2 cloves garlic crushed
1/2-1 qt. stock (Gayelord's vegetable broth)
1-2 tablespoon miso
1/4 cup chopped celery leaves (optional)
2 teaspoons molasses
1-2 teaspoons Spike

    Saute onions and garlic in butter over medium heat in a large saucepan for about 10 minutes. Add the rest of the ingredients and bring to a boil. Reduce heat and simmer for 5 to 10 minutes. Can serve with croutons.

Turkey Meat Loaf

1 pound extra lean ground turkey
1 large onion, finely chopped
1/4 cup natural bran
1 slice whole wheat bread, crumbled (or 1/2 cup Rice crispies)
1/2 teaspoon thyme
1 teaspoon Spike
dash of Worcestershire sauce
1 cup tomato juice or tomato sauce
1 egg, lightly beaten
1 tablespoon chopped fresh herbs-thyme, rosemary, savory, sage, parsley (optional)

    In a mixing bowl, combine all ingredients. Turn into 9x5-inch loaf pan or baking dish. Bake in 350 degree oven for 45 minutes, or until brown and firm to the touch.

Homemade Applesauce
6 apples
handful raisins
1/2 cup water or apple juice
honey to taste
1/2 teaspoon cinnamon
1/4 teaspoon nutmeg
1/4 teaspoon allspice
1/4 teaspoon cloves

Core apples and cut into chunks. Add remaining ingredients including enough honey to sweeten to taste. Bring to a boil and then simmer until tender. Mash with a fork or potato masher. Lemon lends a nice bit of zip to the flavor.

Sprout Salad with Peaches
sprouts
peaches
almond slices

On a bed of sprouts, add some peaches with their juice. Sprinkle a few almond slices on top.

Miso Dessert Balls
1/2 cup peanut butter
1/2 cup honey
1/4 cup carob powder
1/4 cup milk powder (or milk substitute whey powder)
1/4 cup wheat germ
1/4 cup chopped almonds
1/4 cup sunflower seeds
1 1/2 teaspoon miso
1/2 teaspoon cinnamon

Combine all ingredients and mix throughly. Roll into bite size balls. Refrigerate.

Thursday

Apple Bran Muffin
1 cup whole wheat flour

3/4 cup wheat bran
1/4 teaspoon salt
1/2 teaspoon baking soda
1/4 teaspoon nutmeg
1/4 teaspoon cinnamon
1/2 cup finely chopped apple
1/4 cup raisins
1/4 cup chopped nuts
1 cup buttermilk
1 beaten egg
1/4 cup molasses
1 tablespoon oil
1/2 teaspoon maple flavor

Preheat oven to 350 degrees. Grease a 12-cup muffin pan. Toss flour, bran, salt, soda, nutmeg cinnamon together with a fork.

Stir in apples, raisins, and nuts. Combine the liquid ingredients. Stir the liquid ingredients into the dry with a few swift strokes. Pour into greased muffin cups, filling them at least 2/3 full, and bake for 25 minutes. Makes 12.

Cottage Cheese Sandwich

1/2 cup creamed cottage cheese
1/6 cup wheat germ
1/2 tbs. green chillies
1/8 tsp. oregano leaves
1/8 tsp. basil leaves
2 tsp. finely chopped onion
dash salt
dash Tabasco (optional)
tomato slices
alfalfa sprouts

Mix first 8 ingredients together well. Put mound of mixture on a slice of whole wheat bread or toast. Top with a tomato slice and sprouts. Can have an open face sandwich or closed.

Pressure Cooked Stew

1 pound lean chicken, turkey, fish or ham, cut into 1-inch cubes
1 tablespoon olive oil
3 cups water with vegetable broth added

1 large diced potato
2 medium diced carrots
1 onion diced
3 cloves garlic crushed
1 bay leaf
1 teaspoon soy sauce
1/4 Worcestershire
2 tablespoons whole wheat flour
1/2 cup cold water

Shake the 1/2 cup cold water and flour in tightly covered container. Set aside.

Cook and stir meat in olive oil in a pressure cooker until meat is browned, about 15 minutes. Add the water. Pressure cook by bringing it to a rock and let it gently rock for 30 minutes. Take off heat. Let off steam properly. Add the rest of the ingredients and let it get back to a rock for 7 minutes. Remove from heat. Let off steam properly. Stir in the flour mixture. You can use a strainer to remove any lumps. Bring to a boil. Serves 5 or 6.

Cookies
1/2 cup better butter
1 cup brown sugar
1 egg
1-2 teaspoons vanilla
1 cup whole wheat flour
1 cup oat flour (add one cup whole oats to a blender)
1 1/2 teaspoon baking powder

Beat first 4 ingredients until creamy. Add rest of the ingredients and mix well. Place about a teaspoon full of dough for each cookie on a cookie sheet. Bake at 350 degrees for about 8 minutes or until cookies puff up light brown.

Other Cookie Ideas:
-1/4 cup peanut butter. Might need to add 1 teaspoon of flour extra.
-1/2 cup chocolate chips or carob chips
-1/4 cup chopped almonds, walnuts, or pecans
-1/4 cup chopped dates, prunes, or raisins

Friday

Turkey Bacon Sandwich
4 strips turkey bacon cooked
tomato slices
red onion slice
alfalfa sprouts
2 pieces whole wheat bread
Spread: equal parts yogurt and mayonnaise

Spinach & Bean sprout Salad
8 ounces spinach
16 ounces bean sprouts or alfalfa sprouts
croutons (optional)

Sesame Dressing
1/4 cup soy sauce
2 tablespoons toasted sesame seeds
2 tablespoon finely chopped onion
1/2 teaspoon honey
1/4 teaspoon pepper
      Mix all ingredients.
Variations:
-grated carrots
-grated cheese
-cooked noodles
-diced egg
-chopped apples
-cut up dried fruit
-avocado
-nuts
-onions
-crushed bacon
-tomatoes
-any vegetables

Crab Dinner
      Fry in a small amount of olive oil and butter: imitation crab
(pollock fish), diced onions, garlic, sliced mushrooms, bell pepper,

ginger. Sprinkle sunflower seeds or crushed almonds on top before serving.

Variations: bamboo shoots, olives, green chili, Spike seasoning

Fruited Bulgur Pilaf
1 tablespoon "better butter"
1 medium onion chopped
1 cup bulgur uncooked
1/4 teaspoon dill weed
1/4 teaspoon oregano
1/2 teaspoon salt (optional)
1/4 teaspoon pepper
1 tablespoon parsley chopped
chopped apricots, dates and raisins to taste
2 cups water with 1 tablespoon miso mixed in it

     Melt butter in large skillet. Add bulgur and vegetables. Stir constantly until vegetables are tender and bulgur is golden. Add the rest of the ingredients. Bring to a boil. Stir. Reduce heat and simmer 15 minutes.

Italian Cold Vegetables
Using up leftover vegetables (i.e. broccoli, cauliflower, Chile peppers, mushrooms, carrots, zucchini, all beans). Just make sure they haven't been overcooked.
Sprinkle with small amount of marinade from:
1/2 cup olive oil
1/2 cup apple cider vinegar
1/2 tsp. basil
1/2 tsp. oregano leaves
1/2 chopped onion
1 chopped clove garlic
1/4 tsp. sea salt
1/2 tsp dry mustard
1 tsp. paprika
1 tbs. honey

Banana Pudding
5 ripe bananas
4 oz low fat cream cheese

3/4 cup yogurt
1 tsp. vanilla
2 tbs. lemon juice
> Blend all ingredients. Chill.

Saturday

Mexican Omelet

3 eggs scrambled
salsa
grated cheese (optional)
Spray Pam in a frying pan. Add the scrambled eggs. Cover and cook over medium low heat until almost set. Flip. Add salsa to top of eggs and spread. Can add a bit of grated cheese. Put cover back on. Finish cooking. Remove lid. Fold the omelet in half.

Textured Tofu

(The day before, slice firm tofu and pat dry. Freeze separately.) Drop frozen tofu into boiling water. Take out when it's been defrosted. When cool enough to touch, ring out and pat dry. Set aside.

Tofu Steak

In a baggie, add:
1/4 cup water
1 teaspoon vegetable broth
dash Spike
dash poultry seasoning
Add tofu to baggie and marinade.
Dip tofu in a beaten egg.
Then bread in equal parts of whole wheat flour and corn meal.
Fry in small amount of olive oil.

Turkey Sausage Pizza

Pizza Dough
1 pound ripe tomatoes, blanched, seeded ,chopped, and drained as much as possible
Lite Salt & pepper
4 ounces soy cheese, thinly sliced
1 teaspoon dried basil

1/2 teaspoon oregano
1/2 teaspoon parsley
1 onion sliced fine
mushrooms sliced fine (opt.)
4 tablespoon Parmesan cheese
1 tablespoon olive oil

Prepare the pizza dough. Spread the tomatoes almost to the edge, and season well. Cover with the thinly sliced mozzarella; onions, mushrooms, then top with the basil, parsley, oregano, and Parmesan cheese. Sprinkle a little olive oil over the top, and place in a preheated hot oven (450 degrees) for 20 minutes, or until the dough has cooked through and the cheese has melted. Serve.

Pizza Dough
1/2 tablespoon dried yeast
1/2 teaspoon sucanat (sugar cane)
2/3 cup warm water
2 cups whole wheat flour
1 teaspoon Lite Salt
2 tablespoon olive oil

Dissolve yeast with the sugar in 3 to 4 tablespoons of warm water. Leave for 5 to 10 minutes in a warm place (until frothy). Put the flour and salt into a warm bowl; make a well in the center, and pour in the yeast mixture, water, and oil. Mix until it forms a soft dough, adding a bit of warm water if necessary. Turn out onto a floured surface, and knead well for about 5 minutes. Place dough in a floured bowl and cover with a damp cloth. Leave in a warm place until it doubles -about 1 1/2 to 2 hours. Knead lightly. Roll out or press into a pizza pan or baking tray. Pat gently so it fits, with the edges a bit higher.

Banana Waldorf
2 cups diced banana
1 1/2 cups diced apple
1 cup diced celery
1/2 cup chopped walnuts
1/2 cup raisins
1/2 cup yogurt
1 tablespoon lemon juice

Use well-chilled fruit. Combine all ingredients. Mix well and serve on top of fresh spinach leaves or alfalfa sprouts. Yields 6 small servings.

Chinese Chews

1/4 cup butter
1 1/2 cups hulled sesame seeds (or: 3/4 cup sesame seeds, 1/4 crushed almonds, 1/4 cup coconut)
3/4 cup dry milk (or whey milk substitute)
1/6 cup wheat germ
1/2 cup honey
1 to 2 tsp. vanilla
2 tsp. brewers yeast (optional)

Melt butter in skillet. Add sesame seeds and lightly toast, stirring often. Stir in powder milk and wheat germ. Add honey and vanilla mixing well. Continue to cook for about 7 to 8 minutes, stirring constantly. Scoop and press lightly into a greased cookie sheet. Cool and cut into squares.

Sunday

Anner's Blender Pancakes

1 ripe banana
1 egg
1/2 cup flour (wheat, oat, buckwheat)
2 teaspoon baking powder (without alum as an ingredient)
1/2 teaspoon maple flavoring (optional)

Blend the banana, egg, and flavoring in a blender. Add the dry ingredients. Fry as normal in Pam; covering the pan while cooking on the first side.

Humus

1/2 onion, chopped
1 clove garlic crushed
1 tablespoon olive oil
dash cumin
1 teaspoon basil
1/2 teaspoon oregano
2 tablespoon parsley, chopped fine

juice of 1 lemon
1/4 cup sesame seed butter (tahini optional)
3 cups cooked garbanzo beans, mashed
salt to taste

Saute onion and garlic in oil until onion is transparent. Add cumin and cook until fragrant. Add herbs at the last moment, cooking just enough to soften parsley. Mix with the lemon and mashed beans and tahini, stirring together thoroughly. Makes about 3 cups.

Candy Carrots
1/2 pound fresh carrots
honey
chopped almonds

Cut carrots into 2 1/2x1/4 -inch strips. Place carrots in a microwave bowl. Drizzle honey over top. Sprinkle almonds. Cook on high for about 6 minutes in the microwave.

No Fuss Turkey
Clean turkey. Place in a turkey pan. Spread a bit of canola oil over the top and cover tightly with lid or foil. Cook turkey for the amount of time needed based upon the weight of the bird.

Seasoned Bulgur
To 3 cups cooked bulgur, add:
1 1/2 tablespoon vegetable broth
raisins
sunflower seeds
2 teaspoons Spike

Mix together and warm in the microwave.

Orange and Onion Salad
2 oranges
1 diced avocado (optional)
1 grapefruit
1 small red onion, thinly sliced and separated into rings
1/3 cup yogurt
2 tablespoons chopped walnuts (optional)
salad greens or spinach leaves
salt and pepper to taste

Peel and section the fruit. Cut each section into two or three pieces and put in a salad bowl. Add all the juices from the oranges and grapefruit to the onion. Add avocado. Pour yogurt over mixture, toss and chill. Sprinkle with nuts, salt and pepper and serve on salad greens.

A SAMPLING OF DRINKS AND SOUPS THAT CAN BE MADE FROM YOUR HIGH SPEED BLENDER

Carrot and Fruit Medley

1/2 cup pineapple with juice, chilled
1/2 cup carrots
1/2 medium banana
1/4 orange, including white part of peel
1/4-inch slice lemon, peeled
1/4 medium apple
1 cup ice cubes
Place all ingredients in the blender in the order listed. Blend for 1 to 1 1/2 minutes, until smooth. Serve immediately. Makes 2 cups.

Carrot Raisin Drink

3/4 cup carrots
3/4 cup vanilla low-fat yogurt
1/4 cup raisins
1 cup ice cubes
Place all ingredients in blender in the order listed. Blend for 1 to 1 1/2 minutes, until smooth. Serve immediately. Makes 2 cups.

Citrus Carrot Cocktail

1 cup pineapple with juice, chilled
1/2 cup carrots
1/8-inch slice lemon, with peel
1 cup ice cubes
Place all ingredients in blender in the order listed. Blend for 1 to 1 1/2 minutes, until smooth. Serve immediately. Makes 2 cups.

Banana Orange and Carrot Drink

1/2 banana
1 orange, including white part of peel, quartered

3 baby carrots *or* 1/4 cup carrots
1/4 cup celery
1/2 cup cranberry juice
1 teaspoon honey *or* other sweetener, to taste
1 cup ice cubes
Place all ingredients in blender in the order listed. Blend for 1 1/2 to 2 minutes, until smooth. Serve immediately. Makes 2 cups.

Banana Cantaloupe Carrot Cooler
1 banana
1/2 cup cantaloupe
1/4 cup carrot
1/2 kiwi, peeled
1/4 orange, including white part of peel
1/4 lemon, peeled
1 tablespoon honey *or* other sweetener, to taste
1/8 teaspoon nutmeg
1/2 cup pineapple juice
1/4 cup water
1 cup ice cubes
Place all ingredients in the blender in the order listed. Blend for 1 1/2 to 2 minutes, until smooth. Serve immediately. Makes 2 1/2 cups.

Carrot Orange and Apple
1 medium carrot
1 orange, including white part of peel
1/2 apple
1 cup pineapple juice
1/2 cup ice cubes
Place all ingredients in blender in the order listed. Blend for 1 to 1 1/2 minutes, until smooth. Serve immediately. Makes 2 cups.

Hot Mixed Vegetables
1 large tomato, quartered
1/4 cup celery
1/2 clove garlic
1/2 green onion
1/4 cup carrots
1/4 cup water, hot

Place all ingredients in blender in the order listed. Blend for 2 to 3 minutes, until smooth. Serve immediately. Makes 1 cup.

Mixed Fruit Smoothie
1/2 cup frozen strawberries, sweetened
1 banana
1/2 orange, including white part of peel
1/4 cup peaches, frozen
1/2 cup plain yogurt
1/4 cup ice cubes
Place all ingredients in blender in the order listed. Blend for 1 to 1 1/2 minutes, until smooth. Serve immediately. Makes 2 1/2 cups.

Cranberry Apple Drink
1 cup cranberry juice cocktail
1 apple, quartered
1 orange, including white part of peel, quartered
1/2 cup ice cubes
Place all ingredients in blender in the order listed. Blend for 1 to 1 1/2 minutes, until smooth. Serve immediately. Makes 3 cups.

Cantaloupe Pineapple and Banana Cooler
1/2 cup cantaloupe
1/2 cup pineapple with juice, chilled
1/2 medium banana
1/8 inch slice lemon, with peel
1/2 cup cranberry juice
1 tablespoon honey *or* other sweetener, to taste
3/4 cup ice cubes
Place all ingredients in blender in the order listed. Blend for 1 to 1 1/2 minutes, until smooth. Serve immediately. Makes 2 1/2 cups.

Peach Banana Almond Smoothie
1/4 cup peaches, frozen
1/2 medium banana
1/8 teaspoon almond extract
2 tablespoons skim milk
1 tablespoon fructose *or* other sweetener, to taste
1 1/2 teaspoons oat bran

1/2 cup ice cubes
Place all ingredients in blender in the order listed. Blend for 1 to 1 1/2 minutes, until smooth. Serve immediately. Makes 1 cup.

Kiwi Cooler
1/2 kiwi fruit, peeled
1/4 ripe banana
1/2 cup frozen strawberries, sweetened
1/4 cup pineapple juice
1 teaspoon fructose *or* other sweetener, to taste
1 cup ice cubes
Place all ingredients in blender in the order listed. Blend for 1 to 1 1/2 minutes, until smooth. Serve immediately. Makes 2 cups.

Tropical Tofu Smoothie
5 ounces tofu
1/2 cup frozen strawberries
1/2 cup pineapple juice
1/2 teaspoon pure vanilla extract
1/2 teaspoon coconut flavoring
1 teaspoon honey *or* other sweetener, to taste (optional)
Place all ingredients in blender in the order listed. Blend for 1 to 1 1/2 minutes, until smooth. Serve immediately. Makes 2 cups.

Cranberry Citrus Punch
3/4 cup cranberry juice cocktail
1/2 orange, including white part of peel
1/4 cup pineapple
1/4 ripe banana
1/4 cup sweetened strawberries, frozen
1/2 cup club soda
Place all ingredients in blender in the order listed. Blend for 1 to 1 1/2 minutes, until smooth. Serve immediately. Makes 2 1/2 cups.

Grapefruit and Kiwi Drink
1/4 pink grapefruit, peeled
1/2 kiwi fruit, peeled
1/2 cup pineapple juice
1 tablespoon fructose *or* other sweetener, to taste

1/2 cup ice cubes
Place all ingredients in blender in the order listed. Blend for 1 to 1 1/2 minutes, until smooth. Serve immediately. Makes 1 1/4 cups.

Banana Raisin Shake
1 banana
1/4 cup raisins
1/4 cup skim milk
1/4 teaspoon honey
1 cup ice cubes
Place all ingredients in blender in the order listed. Blend for 1 to 1 1/2 minutes, until smooth. Serve immediately. Makes 1 cup.

Strawberry Banana Malt
1/2 cup whole frozen strawberries
1/8 ripe banana
1/2 cup skim milk
1 tablespoon malted milk
1 tablespoon fructose *or* other sweetener, to taste
1/2 teaspoon lemon juice
1/4 cup ice cubes
Place all ingredients in blender in the order listed. Blend for 1 to 1 1/2 minutes, until smooth. Serve immediately. Makes 1 1/2 cups.

Banana Lemonade
1/2 ripe banana
1/2 lemon, peeled
1 cup pineapple juice
1 tablespoon fructose *or* other sweetener, to taste
1/2 cup ice water
1 cup ice cubes
Place all ingredients in blender in the order listed. Blend for 1 to 1 1/2 minutes, until smooth. Serve immediately. Makes 3 cups.

Banana Split Shake
1/2 banana
1/2 cup frozen strawberries
1/4 cup skim milk
1/4 teaspoon rum extract (optional)

1 teaspoon pure vanilla extract
1 tablespoon fructose *or* other sweetener, to taste
1/2 cup ice cubes
Place all ingredients in blender in the order listed. Blend for 1 1/2 to 2 minutes, until smooth. Serve immediately. Makes 1 cup.

Apple Ginger Snap

1/2 cup apple cider
1/4 golden delicious apple
1/4 cup pineapple
1/8 teaspoon ginger root
1 1/4 cups ice cubes
Place all ingredients in blender in the order listed. Blend for 1 to 1 1/2 minutes, until smooth. Serve immediately. Makes 2 1/4 cups.

Tomato Lime Blush

1/2 lime, peeled
1 large tomato *or* 3/4 cup tomato juice
2 tablespoons fructose *or* other sweetener, to taste
1/2 cup water
1/2 cup ice cubes
Place all ingredients in blender in the order listed. Blend for 1 to 1 1/2 minutes, until smooth. Serve immediately. Makes 1 2/3 cups.

Celery Radish and Pineapple Perfection

1/2 cup celery
1/3 cup radishes
3/4 cup fresh *or* canned pineapple
1/2 cup pineapple juice, chilled
1 cup ice cubes
Place all ingredients in the Total Nutrition Center container in the order listed. Secure complete 2-part lid by locking under tabs. Move black speed control lever to HIGH. Lift black lever to ON position and allow machine to run for 1 to 1 1/2 minutes, until smooth. Serve immediately. Makes 2 cups.

Apple Banana and Sweet Potato Cooler

1 medium sweet potato, cooked, peeled and cooled
1/2 cup skim milk

1 small banana
1/2 yellow delicious apple, cut in half
1/8 teaspoon nutmeg
1 tablespoon honey
1 teaspoon pure vanilla extract
2 cups ice cubes
Place all ingredients in blender in the order listed. Blend for 1 to 1 1/2 minutes, until smooth. Serve immediately. Makes 4 cups.

Fruit and Vegetable Powerhouse
1 cup canned pineapple, with juice, chilled
1/4 medium apple
1/2 small banana
1 tablespoon walnuts
1/2 cup carrots
1/3 cup celery
1 large lettuce leaf
1 large spinach leaf
1 tablespoon raisins
1 small parsley sprig
1 cup ice cubes
Place all ingredients in blender in the order listed. Blend for 1 to 1 1/2 minutes, until smooth. Serve immediately. Makes 1 3/4 cups.

Spinach Cocktail
1 cup pineapple juice, chilled
2 fresh peppermint leaves
1 cup fresh spinach leaves
1/2 cup ice cubes
Place all ingredients in blender in the order listed. Blend for 1 to 1 1/2 minutes, until smooth. Serve immediately. Makes 2 cups.

Butternut Squash with Orange and Ginger
1/4 cup butternut squash, cooked and cooled
1 medium orange, including white part of peel, quartered
1 cup orange juice
1/8 teaspoon fresh ginger, peeled
1/2 cup ice cubes

Place all ingredients in blender in the order listed. Blend for 1 to 1 1/2 minutes, until smooth. Serve immediately. Makes 1 3/4 cups.

Beets with Strawberries and Cranberries
3/4 cup cold cranberry juice
1/4 cup whole cranberry sauce *or* fresh cranberries
1 small beet, steamed
1/4 cup fresh *or* 1/3 cup frozen strawberries
2 teaspoons honey *or* other sweetener, to taste
2/3 cup ice cubes
Place all ingredients in blender in the order listed. Blend for 1 to 1 1/2 minutes, until smooth. Serve immediately. Makes 1 2/3 cups.

Strawberry Yogurt Soup
3 cups strawberries
1/2 cup pineapple juice
1 tablespoon sugar *or* other sweetener, to taste
8 ounces strawberry yogurt
Place all ingredients in blender in the order listed. Blend for 1 to 1 1/2 minutes, until smooth. Serve immediately. Makes 3 1/2 cups.

Gazpacho
1 cup cold tomato juice
1/2 large ripe tomato, quartered
1/2 cup cucumber, peeled
1/4 cup onion
1/2 cup sweet green bell pepper, seeded
1 1/4 tablespoons red wine vinegar
1/2 cup ice cubes
1 drop Tabasco® sauce
Salt and pepper to taste
Place all ingredients in blender in the order listed. Blend for 1 to 1 1/2 minutes, until smooth. Serve immediately. Makes 2 1/2 cups.

Chilled Honeydew Soup
3 cups honeydew melon
1/2 cup white grape juice
1 tablespoon sugar *or* other sweetener, to taste

Place all ingredients in blender in the order listed. Blend for 5 seconds for a chunky soup *or* run an additional 15 seconds for a smoother consistency. Chill and serve. Makes 2 1/2 cups.

Serving Suggestions: Garnish by swirling a dab of sour cream, vanilla yogurt through soup for a striking presentation and additional flavor.

Note: Other melon varieties may be substituted for the honeydew such as cantaloupe and watermelon.

Cold Nectarine Dessert Soup

4 nectarines *or* peaches, pitted and halved
1/2 cup white grape juice
1 tablespoon sugar, honey *or* other sweetener, to taste
Juice of 1/2 lemon
1/8 teaspoon cinnamon

Place all ingredients in blender in the order listed. Blend for 1 to 1 1/2 minutes, until smooth. Serve immediately. Makes 3 1/2 cups.

Serving Suggestions: Swirl a dab of vanilla yogurt into each serving and garnish with a mint leaf.

Broccoli Cheese Soup

1 cup hot milk (regular *or* skim)
1/3 cup lowfat cheddar cheese
1 cup broccoli *or* cauliflower, steamed
1/4 cup onion
1 teaspoon cornstarch
1/4 to 1/2 teaspoon chicken bouillon *or* soup base (optional)

Place all ingredients in blender in the order listed. Blend for 1 to 1 1/2 minutes, until smooth. Serve immediately. Makes 2 cups.

Sweet Pea Soup

1/2 cup frozen peas, thawed
1-inch slice sweet red bell pepper
2-inch slice carrot
1/4 cup onion
1 cup boiling chicken, ham *or* vegetable stock (*or* water)
Dash pepper, oregano, garlic powder *or* salt, to taste

Place all ingredients in blender in the order listed. Blend for 1 to 1 1/2 minutes, until smooth. Serve immediately. Makes 1 1/2 cups.

Optional: Garnish with small cubes of ham *or* crumbled bacon.

Instant Tomato Onion Cheese Soup
1 cup tomatoes, quartered and cored
1/4 cup onion
1/4 to 1/2 cup sharp cheddar *or* Swiss cheese
1 tablespoon tomato paste
1 1/2 teaspoons bouillon *or* other seasoning
1 cup water, boiling
Place all ingredients in blender in the order listed. Blend for 1 to 1 1/2 minutes, until smooth. Serve immediately. Makes 2 1/2 to 3 cups.

PATIENT PROFILE: 79 year old woman came to me with symptoms of chronic fatigue or fibromyalgia. Stiffness, pain, fatigue were overwhelming. This person's physician had no definite diagnosis, but was willing to try antibiotics, COX 2 inhibitors (Celebrex), and/or steroids to reduce pain and swelling in patient. Patient was unwilling to take these drugs, given their numerous side effects. Came to me. I recommended dramatic reduction in bread intake, daily consumption of ½ cup of aloe juice, ½ tablespoon of fish oil daily, vitamin D supplements (5000 iu/d), and cherry syrup (for its anti-inflammatory properties), and increase in fruits and vegetables. Patient began having more regular bowel movements. Within 2 months, patient was mostly recovered. Now, at age 81, mows her own 1 acre lawn all summer and shovels her own snow all winter. Patient was my mother, Margaret Mary Quillin, who is doing very well.

CHAPTER 8
GENERAL RULES FOR WELLNESS

"May you make lots of money, and spend it all on doctor's bills."
famous old gypsy curse

FROM NATURE'S PHARMACY: CURCUMIN. For over 4000 years, Indian people have used curry to season their food and Indian Ayurvedic medicine has used curry as a favorite medicine. Curry is a blend of herbs, like the recipe for chocolate chip cookies...everyone has their own version. Turmeric, red pepper, black pepper, and cumin are common ingredients in curry spice. Turmeric is the bright yellow herb also found in mustard. Turmeric is rich in curcumin, which has active ingredients called curcuminoids. These yellow substances have a list of biological activity that would make any drug company president drool with envy: anti-cancer, anti-arthritic, liver protective, anti-inflammatory, anti-viral, slows Alzheimer's, and treats malaria. Researchers then found that turmeric is poorly absorbed...unless you add black pepper, which dramatically enhances the absorption of turmeric. Note the above 4000 year old recipe for curry mixes turmeric and black pepper. Start using curry and turmeric in many of your foods. You are practicing herbal medicine without a license.

GENERAL TIPS ON WELLNESS

Your body wants to be well. If you feed and care for your body properly, it will probably serve you well for 80 years or more. If ignored or abused, the body can become undependable and painful, causing you to spend more time in doctor's waiting rooms than you care to count. Let's look at some basic ways of encouraging your body's own active healing mechanisms. Consider these "power points". They will provide you a dividend yield of at least 100% per year. Match that with your recent financial investments.

POWER POINTS
USE ADVANCED
HEALTH "RADAR" TESTS

VALUABLE, SCIENTIFICALLY
PROVEN TESTS TO DETECT
POTENTIAL HEALTH ISSUES
Complete male/female panel
Life Extension, Lef.org
800-544-4440
fasting blood glucose & insulin
homocysteine
C reactive protein
vitamin D
fibrinogen
percent body fat Tanita.com
blood pressure home monitor

POWER POINTS
COLON TRANSIT TIME

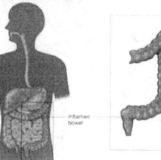

FROM MOUTH TO ANUS
IN 16-24 HOURS (BEETS)
IMPORTANT FOR HEALTH
40% OF IMMUNE SYSTEM

"DEATH BEGINS
IN THE COLON"
Eli Metchnikov, PhD
Nobel prize medicine 1908

ACCOMPLISHED THROUGH:
FIBER, FLUID, EXERCISE TO GUT
NUTRIENTS FOR PERISTALSIS: FOLATE, PROTEIN

HOW DO WE HEAL?

- •"NATURE alone cures."
- •Florence Nightingale, founder of modern nursing, 1900 AD
- •"Natural forces within us are the true healers."
- •Hippocrates, father of modern medicine, 400 BC
- •Germs do not cause disease in the real sense. Something happens in the body to allow the germs to become invasive." Antoine Bechamp, MD, PhD 1900
- •"Each patient carries his own doctor inside him."
- •Albert Schweitzer, MD, Nobel laureate, 1940
- •"The germ is nothing. The 'terrain' is everything."
- •Louis Pasteur, founder of microbiology, 1895
- •"The doctor of the future will give no medicine, but will involve the patient in the proper use of food, fresh air & exercise."
- •Thomas Edison, inventor with over 1000 patents

POWER POINTS
DENTAL HEALTH CRITICAL

LESS SUGAR
BRUSH
DR. PHILLIPS BLOTTING
FLOSS
WATER PIC

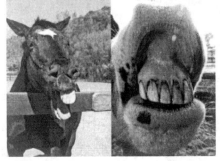

OIL PULLING
1 TABLESPOON SESAME
OIL SWISHED IN MOUTH
15 MINUTES PER DAY
SPIT OUT, RINSE

500 DIFFERENT BACTERIA/FUNGUS IN MOUTH

POWER POINTS
CHANGE YOUR OIL

FATS IN DIET CREATE

FATS IN BODY

REGULATE EVERYTHING

CELL MEMBRANE

GATEKEEPER

COOK WITH: OLIVE AND COCONUT
USE: SESAME, GRAPESEED
SUPPLEMENT WITH: FISH, BORAGE, CLA
USE SPARINGLY: BUTTER
AVOID: HYDROGENATED

POWER POINTS
PUT OUT THE FIRE
ANTIOXIDANT/PROOXIDANT

FREE RADICALS CAUSE
TISSUE DAMAGE, AGING, CANCER

ANTIOXIDANTS SLOW DAMAGE

FOOD: COLORFUL FRUITS & VEG

SUPPLEMENTS: C, E, BETA CAROTENE
LIPOIC ACID, COQ, SELENIUM

ORAC: OXYGEN RADICAL
ABSORBENCE CAPACITY
sponges for free radicals

ORAC/5 GM	
prunes 288	"...reduce risk of diseases of aging by adding high **ORAC** foods to diet." Floyd Horn, PhD, Tufts Univ.
raisins 141	
blueberries 111	
blackberries 101	
garlic 96	*need 3000-5000 ORAC units/day*
kale 88	*(food & supplements)*
cranberries 87	*average US intake 1200 ORAC*
strawberries 76	
spinach raw 60	
plum 47	

POWER POINTS
GET YOUR "D"

VITAMIN D; MOST PEOPLE DEFICIENT
REQUIRED FOR CALCIUM USE: BONES, MUSCLES
"TELEGRAPH" FOR CELL FUNCTIONS
ANTI-CANCER, ANTI-OBESITY, ANTI-DIABETES
ANTI-AGING, ANTI-DEPRESSION

IS SUN EXPOSURE GOOD FOR US?

❧excess sun exposure (free radicals) on fair
skin with excess PUFA diet (vulnerable to
free radicals) with AOX deficient diet=
cataracts, basal & squamous carcin, mac.deg.

✑Lowest incidence of melanoma found in outdoor constr.workers.
Sunnier climates have 50% reduction in risk for most other cancers.
Sun exposure lowers incidence of depression, auto-immune diseases.
Sunlight (UVB) generates 10,000 iu/day vit.D semi-naked adult.
RDA vit.D=400 iu, NEW REC: 1000-2000 IU ADULTS
Most older Americans deficient in vitamin D
Vitamin D effective against infections, cancer, heart disease,
osteoporosis, depression, auto-immune diseases.
40,000 iu (1000 mcg=1 mg) toxic

Vieth. R., Am.J.Clin.Nutr., vol.69, no.5, p.842,May 1999; Am.J.Clin.Nutr.,vol.77, p.204 Jan.2003

POWER POINTS
SPICE UP YOUR LIFE

PRACTICING HERBAL MEDICINE WITHOUT LICENSE

POWER POINTS

GO FOR THE COLOR

<u>COLORFUL PIGMENTS HAVE</u>

CAROTENOIDS

BIOFLAVONOIDS

ANTIOXIDANTS

BIOREGULATORS

POWER POINTS
WHOLE FOOD
PLANT BASED
LOW GLYCEMIC DIET

LOOKING AT A HEALTHY MEAL PLATE

tomato,spinach,carrot,peppers,
fruit.broccoli.cabbage,onion,etc

fish, wild game, poultry,
lean beef,eggs,br.yeast
beans, dairy,spirulina,kelp

1/3
raw fr/veg

1/3
lo fat/hi pro

1/3
cooked whole plant food

oatmeal,beans,bread,tortilla
pasta,yams,nuts,grains,
legumes,cooked vegetables

POWER POINTS
KEEP MOVING

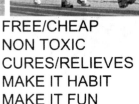

FREE/CHEAP
NON TOXIC
CURES/RELIEVES
MAKE IT HABIT
MAKE IT FUN

EXERCISE: how to

Daily

1) warm up (light rowing, movement)

2) strengthen (swim, weights, calisthenics)

3) stretch

4) aerobic (12 minutes being winded)

5) cool down, Tai Chi

POWER POINTS
DEVELOP COPING
TECHNIQUES FOR THE
"SPEED BUMPS" OF LIFE

Hans Selye, MD "father of modern stress", Univ. Montreal
1500 technical articles, 32 books, 42 honor.fellowships
STRESS, DISTRESS (-), EUSTRESS (+), HPA axis

1) Stress is like tension on violin strings, need some music

2) Lean on a "Higher Power"

3) Know your capacity: racehorse vs. turtle

Deepak Chopra,MD "Every cell in your body
is eavesdropping on your thoughts."

POWER POINTS
NUTRITION SUPPLEMENTS

FATS	MINERALS	PHYTOCHEMICALS
EPA, GLA	MAGNESIUM	BETA SITOSTEROL
	CHROMIUM	VINPOCETINE
VITAMINS		BILBERRY
D	ANTIOXIDANTS	ZEAXANTHIN
E	COQ	FUCOIDAN
B-12	LIPOIC ACID	GREEN TEA
FOLATE	RESVERATROL	ELLAGIC ACID

WHY SUPPLEMENTS ARE VALUABLE: depleted soils,
highly refined foods, stress, excess toxins, surviving vs
thriving, "beyond deficiency" functions of nutrients

recommend: ImmunoPower EZ at GettingHealthier.com

POWER POINTS
HEALTHY PLEASURES

DARK CHOCOLATE	FRIENDSHIPS
NAPS/SIESTA	SUNSHINE
RED WINE	HOT SAUCE
LAUGHTER	MUSIC
SEX	VACATIONS

POWER POINTS
A DOZEN LAUGHS A DAY

ALLOWS US TO TOLERATE THE ABSURD
DRAMATICALLY LOWERS STRESS
REGULATES IMMUNE FUNCTIONS
INTERNAL "JOGGING"

WHAT DO THESE "LONGEVITY EXPERTS" HAVE IN COMMON?

Groucho Marx 87 yr

MILTON BERLE 93 YR

BOB HOPE 100 YR

Art Linkletter 1912-? 93 yr

Jack LaLanne 1915-? 91 yr

GEORGE BURNS 99 YR

POWER POINTS
YOU MAY HAVE 100% COMPLIANCE ON THESE PRINCIPLES...
BUT YOU'RE STILL GONNA DIE

MAKE EACH DAY A MASTERPIECE TO EXPRESS AND EXPERIENCE THE CREATOR

DETOXIFICATION

TOXINS: lower immune functions & damage DNA

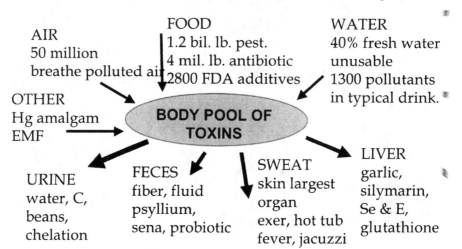

AIR
50 million
breathe polluted air

FOOD
1.2 bil. lb. pest.
4 mil. lb. antibiotic
2800 FDA additives

WATER
40% fresh water
unusable
1300 pollutants
in typical drink.

OTHER
Hg amalgam
EMF

BODY POOL OF TOXINS

URINE
water, C,
beans,
chelation

FECES
fiber, fluid
psyllium,
sena, probiotic

SWEAT
skin largest
organ
exer, hot tub
fever, jacuzzi

LIVER
garlic,
silymarin,
Se & E,
glutathione

COMPLETE HOST DEFENSE MECHANISMS

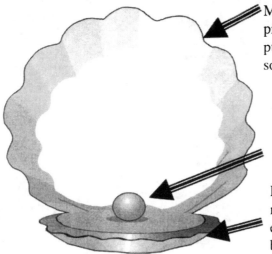

METAPHYSICAL
protection: spirit, love,
purpose, expression,
social network, touching

person's life force

PHYSICAL protection:
nutrition, avoid toxins,
exercise, sun, fresh air,
body alignment

PATIENT PROFILE: BEAT ENDSTAGE TUBERCULOSIS

True story. The number one cause of death throughout most of the 19th century was tuberculosis. Galen Clark went to Yosemite Valley to die of endstage tuberculosis at age 42 in the fall of 1856. His doctor told him that coughing up chunks of his lungs meant he had up to 2-6 months to live. There was no cure for this disease. Clark reasoned that "If I'm going to die soon, then I'm going to die in Yosemite, the prettiest place I've ever seen." He got happy. Scientists now tell us that happiness brings on the flow of endorphins, which supercharge our immune system and may slow down cancer.

Next, Galen Clark carved his own tombstone, thus accepting his mortality, a ritual that would give us all a better appreciation of our finite time on earth. He then started eating what was available in Yosemite in those days; clean and lean wild game, mountain trout, nuts, berries, vegetables, and lots of clean water. No sugar and no dairy products. He then began doing what he wanted to do, hiking and creating trails, in the place he treasured the most, Yosemite Valley. He didn't die 6 months later, but rather 54 years later, just shy of his 96th birthday. He bolstered his "non-specific host defense mechanisms" with good thoughts and good nutrition.

GALEN CLARK 1814-1910

"I went to the mountains to take my chances of dying or getting better; which I thought were about even."

CHAPTER 9
WEIGHT LOSS
SAFE, NATURAL AND PERMANENT

I've gained a few pounds around the middle. The only lower-body garments I own that still fit me comfortably are towels.

Dave Barry, comedian

FROM NATURE'S PHARMACY: HEALTHY FATS THAT MAKE YOU THIN: EPA, GLA, CLA. Americans eat too much fat and the wrong kind of fat. Yet, there is equally convincing evidence that we  have serious fatty acid deficiencies. Bad fats include hydrogenated, or trans fats, with no known safety level. Good fats include EPA from fish oil, GLA from borage or primrose oil, and CLA from the meat and milk of ruminant animals grazed on green grass. Each of these fats has merit in your diet and/or supplement program. Fish oil may prevent or reverse early stages of heart disease, dysplasias (pre-cancerous conditions), depression, auto-immune disease (like multiple sclerosis and arthritis), diabetes, skin problems, and obesity, according to Andrew Stoll, MD of Harvard. GLA is a powerful anti-inflammatory fat. CLA was a true surprise for the researchers when they found that something in hamburger could have anti-cancer activity. When ruminants (cows, sheep, deer, buffalo, etc.) eat green grass, the linoleic acid (which promotes cancer) in the stomach is converted to conjugated linoleic acid, which has been shown to slow or delay cancer and may reduce fat deposits in humans. Grass fed animals have 500% more CLA than grain fed animals.

OBESITY INCREASE THE RISK FOR:

cancer

heart disease

diabetes

>renal fail, blind, gangrene, heart disease

stroke

Alzheimer's

OBESITY PROVES IMPACT OF
DIETARY ENDOCRINOLOGY

NUTRITION: Eat and enjoy your food. Do not skip meals. Concentrate on foods high in fiber and fluid (vegetables, fruit, grains, legumes, water). Minimize pastries, alcohol, high sugar, and fat foods. Calories *do* count! To avoid overeating, have soups and salads 20 minutes before mealtime and drink a glass of water just before the meal. Eat until satisfied, not stuffed. If consuming less than 1000 calories per day (medical supervision recommended) take a vitamin and mineral supplement daily.

EXERCISE: This is essential to successful weight control. Must be fun, vigorous, and regular (minimum 3 times/week at 1 hour each session). Strive for improvement in strength, flexibility, and cardiovascular fitness. Start gradually with non-stress bearing routines like biking, swimming, and fast walking. Join supportive exercise groups. Exercise improves mental and physical health, elevates basal metabolism for fast calorie burning, prevents disease, and lengthens life. Functional activities of work and play count, too.

"The only exercise some people get is coughing." *Robert Orben, comedian*

What if I had a "miracle cure" in my pocket that would help you:

- lose weight
- eat more without gaining weight, since muscle cells burn 50 times more calories than fat cells
- increase the number of insulin receptors, thus reversing insulin resistance
- lower fasting blood glucose
- reduce serum lipids, i.e. cholesterol and triglycerides
- detoxify the body through sweat and other means
- "cook" off germs by raising body temperature
- relax with the flow of endorphins
- stimulate the brain to be more alert and intelligent
- elevate immune functions, thus protecting you against infections and cancer
- encourage regular bowel movements
- bring more life-giving oxygen to the cells
- strengthen the bones to reverse and prevent osteoporosis
- enhance posture and muscles surrounding the back
- improve sleep
- increase self-esteem
- strengthen the heart
- and much, much more

This miracle cure can be free or very inexpensive. For most people, there are no negative side effects and no addictions. You never have to worry about getting this "prescription" refilled because it is wherever you are. Would you be interested in such a miracle drug? Well, it's here and waiting for you. It's called exercise.

Our ancestors were active outdoorsmen. They walked, ran, hunted, farmed, worked, cut wood, ground grain and more. Our bodies are built for regular movement. We function better and live longer and healthier when we have a regular program of exercise. Yet, 30% of Americans admit to getting no exercise, while 60% get very little movement. More than coincidentally, these number are the same for the percentage of Americans who are medically obese (30%) and those who are overweight (60%). To boil this chapter down to two powerful sound bites:

❖ **"You've got to move it to lose it."**
❖ **"Use it or lose it."**

Make sure that you have your doctor's okay to begin your exercise program. Try to make your exercise part of your daily routine. The old saying "No pain, no gain" may apply for the first few weeks if you have been sedentary for quite some time. Waking up your dormant muscles involve some discomfort. Hang in there. It's worth the effort to do 30 to 60 minutes of exercise daily. Try to make exercise time, play time. Remember the fun you had as a child playing

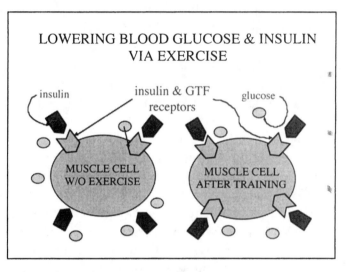

LOWERING BLOOD GLUCOSE & INSULIN VIA EXERCISE

skip rope, skateboarding, biking, or Marco Polo in the pool. You may not have the same endurance and flexibility as you did in your younger days, but you can still make exercise fun. Watch how excited a dog gets when you bring out the leash for a walk.

Essential components of an exercise program:

1) Warm up. Spend 5 minutes doing some simple stretching. Learn from yoga videos how to limber up the body.

2) Cardio-vascular endurance. Spend 15 minutes doing something that gets you sweating; i.e. brisk walking, running, biking, rowing machine, cross country skiing machine, pilates, etc.

3) Strength training. Doing push up, pull ups, dips, or using weights helps to build muscle mass which burns 50 times more calories than fat cells. Exercise forces the body to make more insulin receptors on the cell membrane, which makes insulin more effective in your body.

4) Cool down. Spend 5 minutes doing more stretching.

BEHAVIOR MODIFICATION: Eat and chew slowly. Put your fork down between each bite. Allow at least 20 minutes for each meal. Use small plates. Keep leftovers out of sight. Keep snack foods out of your house. Leave a bite on each plate to signal satiety. Put leftovers in refrigerator, not in your mouth. Know the environmental cues (e.g. TV, reading, driving) which make you eat. Avoid these cues or substitute other behaviors like crafts. Eat only at the table at mealtime. Pre-plan meals. Do not shop when hungry. Enjoy your meals with candles, music, nice clothes, etc. Store food in opaque containers. Plan soups and casseroles for leftovers. Keep a written record of what & how much you eat & mood at that time.

Nearly all women (97%) and most men (68%) crave certain foods. If you can harness your food cravings, then weight control and the waist line you have been imagining is just around the corner. There are appetite suppressant drugs, most of which have major side effects. Remember the phen-fen disaster of the 1990s. Fenfluramine was the appetite suppressant part of the drug combination that induced weight loss. Fenfluramine was removed from the market in 1997 by the FDA because it caused heart valve problems, including heart attacks. There are better ways of controlling your food cravings.

You crave what you eat. Researchers find that if you can get past the first few days of establishing a new healthier food to crave, then you will find yourself in control of your appetite. Give away the junk food in your kitchen. Don't eat it all tonight thinking that you don't want to waste that food. Bring in foods recommended in this book for your new snacking food. Offer yourself a reward when you make it past the first week of using new "power" foods.

Nuts and water. Eat a tablespoon of nuts and drink two glasses of water. Both will fill you up without filling you out. Water and nuts are great appetite appeasers.

Manage your stress. Many people eat as an outlet for their stress. Find healthier ways of dealing with your stress. Do some exercise. Find a counselor, friend, pastor or rabbi to talk to. Use relaxation CDs and meditation to dissipate the stress. Change your attitude about the problems, or change your venue.

Napping and sleep. Food cravings are more likely to happen in tired people. Get enough sleep at night. Take afternoon naps when possible.

Distract yourself for 15 minutes. Typical cravings last 10 minutes. Do something else, like listen to music, call someone, meditate, take a walk, surf the internet.

Indulge yourself on occasion. Once in a while, allow yourself that food that you crave, then work it off in exercise. Make a deal with yourself. "If I eat it, then I must burn it off."

Avoidance helps. Take a different route home from work, rather than driving by your favorite pizza or ice cream joint.

ATTITUDE: Never say "diet". This is a lifetime program of healthy living. Set realistic goals and reward yourself (not with food) when you reach these goals. Deal with the moods (e.g. depression, boredom, self-pity) which provoke an appetite. Talk to friends, or seek professional counseling. Accept total responsibility for your life and weight. Seek the support of friends and family. No one can sabotage your efforts if you don't want them to. If you expect someone or something else to do it for you, or a "cure" for overweight, or immediate results; then you will likely fail at losing. Be prepared for thinness, you will be healthier and happier, but life will not be perfect. See yourself as thin. Eat and exercise accordingly. Know the difference between biological hunger and psychological appetite. Subdue the latter. Do not be discouraged or torture yourself after an occasional binge. Reaffirm your desire to be lithe & healthy. Join support groups. Eat your planned food before going to parties & avoid high calorie appetizers OR exercise extra and eat less BEFORE the party to allow for slight overindulgence. You, too, can be lean, attractive, healthy, energetic & long lived.

THE WILD CARDS

So you have done all of the above and you still struggle with a weight problem. There may be some "tricks" or "wild cards" that can help you.

1) DHEA. As we age, our internal production of most hormones declines. DHEA (dehydroepiandrosterone) is manufactured in the adrenals and is the most common hormone in the human body, because it is a precursor (raw materials to make) many other hormones in the body. Most people are seriously deficient in DHEA after age 40. Work with you doctor. Take a blood or saliva test. If your DHEA is low, taking supplements (25-50 mg/day) may be of benefit.

2) THYROID. Again, our output of hormones, like thyroxin from the thyroid gland declines as we age. Low output of thyroxin (hypothyroidism) often shows up as weight loss, fatigue, and pasty skin. Work with your doctor. Maybe iodine supplements will help. Maybe you need a prescription of natural desiccated thyroxin. Boosting your metabolism by getting your blood thyroxin levels improved can often help people into a healthy weight loss pattern.

3) AVOID ARTIFICIAL SWEETENERS. People who consume large amounts of artificial sweeteners (Nutrasweet, saccharin, aspartame) actually gain weight, because the body is eating something sweet but not registering an increase in blood glucose. This false signal affects insulin levels and appetite to increase eating.[1]

4) GET SOME SLEEP. There is evidence that staying up late and excessive exposure to light defies the body's built in signals for daylight and darkness in our daily routines. Get 6 to 9 hours of sleep each night and you are more likely to lose weight.

5) POLLUTION IS PARTLY TO BLAME. A multitude of "hormone disrupters", like Bisphenol A found in soft clear plastics, is a true menace in our body. Do not microwave food in plastic containers. Use stainless steel or glass containers for food and beverage.

PATIENT PROFILE: Patrick Quillin (yes, that's me) was writing a book on health and longevity back in 1985. And I felt terrible while doing it. Sitting at my desk all day left me feeling stiff at the end of the day. "What's wrong with this picture" I said to myself. I started following my own advice. Started doing calisthenics, pull ups, dips, and some free weights. Promised myself that I could not eat breakfast until I had done 1 hour of exercise. Biking, walking, martial arts, swimming, yoga, and rowing machine have all been part of my daily routine. Today, at age 58, my health is great. I don't exercise because I think it might help me live a few years longer. I do it because I feel better immediately. And so will you...

ENDNOTES

[1] Swithers SE, Davidson TL. A role for sweet taste: Calorie predictive relations in energy regulation by rats. Behav Neurosci. 2008 Feb;122(1):161-73.

CHAPTER 10
DIABETES
THE 900 POUND GORILLA IN
AMERICA'S HEALTH CARE CLOSET

"Our way of life is related to our way of death."
The Framingham Study from Harvard University

FROM NATURE'S PHARMACY: Cinnamon

Columbus set sail over the mysterious edge of the ocean in search of spices to cover the smell of decaying food. Until refrigerator were made widely available in 1916 by General Electric, all food had a very short shelf life. Once you picked the plant or killed the animal, the process of decomposition and the rotting smell marched by quickly. The spices of the orient, such as black pepper, turmeric, cinnamon, red peppers, ginger; were greatly prized throughout the world for making food taste and smell better. Only a few bright people had observed that these spices also made the user a bit healthier. Cinnamon is a case in point. Throughout history, cinnamon was a favorite spice mixed with sweets. Grandmas for centuries have made cinnamon apple pie for dessert. Now scientists find that cinnamon can help to lower blood glucose rises. While the data on using cinnamon (or the patented Cinnulin extract) for treating diabetes is mixed, there is clear evidence that cinnamon used regularly as a spice in the diet can make appreciable reductions in blood glucose levels, according to a well respected researcher at the United States Department of Agriculture, Dr. Richard Anderson.[1]

DIABETES: SIMPLE BUT DEADLY IF UNCONTROLLED

At first glance, diabetes appears to be such a simple disease. Too much sugar in the blood. But that simple error creates an avalanche of problems in the body that create havoc with the health of diabetics, especially if they have poor regulation of their blood glucose. Diabetes is such an insidious disease that it is the leading cause of blindness, kidney disease, amputations, and heart disease in the US.[2]

And yet, if properly regulated, diabetes can become a minor limitation in life, which is how baseball legends Jackie Robinson and Catfish Hunter viewed their diabetes. Diabetes did not seriously curtail the accomplishments of diabetics Ray Kroc, multi-billionaire and founder of the McDonald's empire; Hollywood celebrities Jack Benny, Mary Tyler Moore, and Ella Fitzgerald; U.S. Supreme Court Justice Oliver Wendell Holmes (who lived to age 94); and Ron Gillombardo, who at age 45 in 1992 in Barcelona became the oldest man in Olympic history to compete in power lifting. Mr. Gillombardo told the press that, were it not for his diabetes and need to follow a strict diet, he could not have accomplished such an athletic feat at such an age. Diabetes can become a wretched disease for those who ignore it, or an opportunity to make your life into a masterpiece for those who control it.

There is convincing evidence that you can improve quality and quantity of life and reduce complications for nearly all diabetics when using an aggressive nutrition program. Some Type 2 diabetics (non-insulin dependent) may actually have their disease go into complete remission by following these recommendations. This chapter brings empowerment, therapeutic options, hope, wisdom, and a detailed game plan to you, the diabetic, to keep you out of harm's reach and filled with the zest of life.

INCIDENCE OF DIABETES IN US AND WORLD

In 2003, the United States Centers for Disease Control and Prevention stated that "the incidence of diabetes has escalated to epidemic proportions." 23 million Americans now have diabetes, of which 17 million have been diagnosed and the remaining 6 million are "ticking time bombs" waiting for some health calamity before recognizing the disease. Another 16 million have pre-diabetes, which dramatically elevates their risk for eventually deteriorating into full blown diabetes.[3] Undiagnosed diabetics may not receive treatment until something serious happens, like blindness, kidney failure, heart attack, or gangrene sets in. Experts now estimate annual US health care costs for diabetes at $132 billion. Each year in America another

650,000 cases of diabetes are diagnosed. 120 million people around the globe suffer from diabetes. While 20% of Americans overall will develop diabetes in their lifetime, African Americans are twice as likely to develop diabetes compared to Anglos, and Latinos are even more prone toward diabetes than African Americans. All groups are at greater risk for developing diabetes as we age.

CATEGORIES OF DIABETES

Let's make sure that we have the proper terminology for diabetes:

- ♥ Diabetes insipidus: disease of high urine output, possibly caused by lack of the pituitary hormone, anti-diuretic hormone.
- ♥ Diabetes mellitus: (means "siphoning sweetness") metabolic disease of too much glucose in the blood as caused by:

1) Lack of insulin output, type 1 diabetes, juvenile diabetes, Insulin Dependent Diabetes Mellitus (IDDM)

2) Ineffective insulin, meaning there is enough insulin but it does not effectively force glucose into the cells, type 2 diabetes, adult onset diabetes, Non Insulin Dependent Diabetes Mellitus (NIDDM)

WHAT ARE THE COMPLICATIONS OF DIABETES?

Remember, this is a loaded question. The statistics regarding diabetics in America are not very encouraging. However, the diseases that affect the diabetic are started and exaggerated by poor blood glucose control. You can minimize your risk for the following conditions. But be aware that ignoring your diabetes puts you in a high risk category for problems of the:

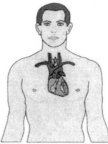

- ♥ Circulatory system, including heart disease, stroke, poor circulation to the feet and hands. 80% of Type 2 diabetics die from heart disease.
- ♥ Shriveling of the tiny blood vessels leading to problems in the eyes, a.k.a. retinopathy. 15 years after diagnosis, 90% of Type 1 and 80% of Type 2 diabetics show some damage to the retina of the eyes.

♥ Kidney complications, or nephropathy. The vast majority of American patients on renal dialysis are diabetics.

♥ Nerve damage, or neuropathy, leading to tingling, painful, "pins & needles" sensations in the hands and feet.

> ♥ Nerve damage to the bladder, intestines, sexual organs, etc. and the consequences of losing the contributions from those organs or regions of the body.
>
> ♥ Ulcers of the leg and foot, which are combined problems of nerves and blood vessels.

WILL THIS PROGRAM IMPROVE MY TYPE 2 DIABETES?

Since 90% of Type 2 diabetics are obese, weight reduction can dramatically improve blood glucose regulation and even cure the diabetes.[4] Obesity may distort the "landing sites" for insulin on the cell membrane, not unlike blowing up a balloon larger than normal and watching the writing on the balloon become distorted. People can dramatically improve blood glucose regulation merely by eating a "hunter gatherer diet" consisting of lean and clean meat (chicken, turkey, fish, lean beef and pork) along with complex carbohydrates rich in soluble fiber (vegetables, nuts, seeds, fruit, legumes) and insoluble fiber (whole grains).

Researcher Dr. Kerin O'Dea in Australia wondered if the modern refined diet of many Aborigines living in Sidney, Australia could cause diabetes. She recruited 10 full blooded male aborigines who had Type 2 diabetes and asked them to return to the "hunter gatherer" diet of their ancestors. All 10 subjects were middle age and overweight. Seven weeks after beginning their ancestral diet, all 10 men had lost an average of 16 pounds in spite of making no effort to reduce weight, all had experienced a 50% drop in blood lipids (lowering their risk for heart disease), and all had such splendid improvement in fasting blood glucose levels that they were considered "cured" of Type 2 diabetes.[5]

Max Gerson, MD was a well-respected German neurosurgeon in the 1920s. He began treating "refractory" diseases of all sorts, including diabetes, lupus, and cancer with a basic program of nutrition and detoxification. Dr. Gerson used his simple program to cure the wife of the famous medical missionary, Dr. Albert Schweitzer, from advanced tuberculosis in 1928, and then cured Schweitzer himself of Type 2 diabetes, allowing Schweitzer to live another 15 years to age 90.[6]

This book will also help at-risk people who want to prevent diabetes. Diabetes is becoming a great concern to the state and federal government because health care costs from Medicare and Medicaid have skyrocketed due to rampant diabetes. The National Institutes of Health sponsored a study, the Diabetes Prevention Program, which showed that little efforts can make a huge difference in diabetes risk. As little as a 5-7% weight loss coupled with small changes in the diet and 30 minutes daily of exercise was able to cut the risk for developing diabetes by 50% in high risk individuals.

BLOOD SUGAR, FOOD SUGAR, AND THE DISEASES OF CIVILIZATION

In the 1930s, a dentist Weston Price, and his wife/nurse, decided to quit their practices and travel the world in the ultimate "Indiana Jones" scientific study and adventure. Traveling on propeller planes to 12 cultures on 5 continents, they found that people who

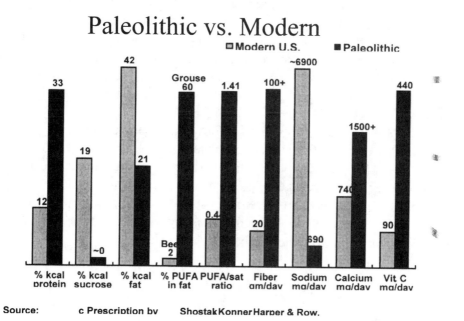

Paleolithic vs. Modern

Source: c Prescription by   Shostak Konner Harper & Row.

consumed their ancestral diet had both good teeth and generally good health. Once these people adopted the "western diet" (Read: refined carbohydrates lacking in fiber) then both the teeth and general health of these varied cultures began to rapidly deteriorate.[7] Diabetes was virtually never seen in people who followed their native ethnic diet.

Drs. Shostak, Eaton, and Konner of Emory University studied the lifestyle of the few remaining "hunter gatherer" cultures around the world and compared their diet to ours, then published this research in the prestigious New England Journal of Medicine and as a book, THE PALEOLITHIC PRESCRIPTION. There is a huge gap between what we modern Americans are currently eating and what our bodies are designed to require.[8] Americans get 19% of our calories from simple carbohydrates, mostly white sugar. Our ancestors got almost no calories from simple carbohydrates, except for the brief harvest time for fruits in the summer and fall. The glycemic index of real fruit usually is much better than the glycemic index of refined sugars. Glycemic index basically tells us how fast the sugar gets into our bloodstream.

TIME RELEASE FOOD SUPPLY

For thousands of years, our ancestors ate foods that slowly released their calories in the process of digestion, to be eventually absorbed into the bloodstream and easily handled by a meager supply of insulin. However, modern Americans have ignored this biological adaptation of our bodies and consume huge amounts of refined carbohydrates to bring about a rush of easily absorbed sugars into the bloodstream.

Fiber in whole foods slows down the absorption of sugar into the bloodstream so that blood glucose stays at a manageable level. With the 140 pounds per year of refined white sugar consumed annually by the average American, and the fact that the most commonly eaten food in America is white bread, we now literally inject sugars into our bloodstream. This is one of the main reasons for the epidemic proportions of diabetes in America.

WHY IS DIABETES SO COMMON?

HUNTER/GATHERER ANCESTORS

healthy blood glucose
60-90 mg%

fat storage

meat
veg.

eyes,brain,etc.

dietary
carb

glycemic
index

blood glucose
levels

energy muscles

abnormal cell
membrane

140 lb/yr sugar
15 bil gal pop
2.7 bil Kr.Cre
#1 white bread
#1 veg.potato
watermelon

unhealthy blood glucose
80-200 mg%

fat storage

eyes,brain,etc.

MODERN AMERICANS

energy for
muscles

Diabetes is one of the more prevalent, lethal, expensive, and easily reversed conditions in America. The vast majority of diabetes is caused by ignoring the basic laws of Nature. Humans need "time release" foods that slowly allow small amounts of carbohydrates to be absorbed into the bloodstream. We are built for activity and get sick when we overeat or develop obesity. 95% of all sugar in the blood is supposed to be burned by the muscles, yet sedentary Americans end up having that sugar linger in the blood until the insulin supply can force the sugar either into storage as glycogen or storage as fat. We have a nutritional need for a wide assortment of nutrients involved in burning sugar in our cell furnaces, not unlike needing spark plugs in your car to burn the gasoline in your engine. These "spark plugs" that are deficient in our Standard American Diet (SAD) include magnesium, chromium, vanadium, and omega-3 fats from fish and flax oils.

Most of our hunter-gatherer ancestors ate a diet consisting of about 1/3 lean animal tissue with the remaining 2/3 of the diet unprocessed plant food; mostly vegetables, some grains, some fruit, nuts, seeds and legumes. If the creature runs, flies, or swims, then it may be about 4% body fat, with obvious exceptions including duck and salmon. Cows, the staple meat of America, do not run, swim, or fly and are about 30-40% body fat after they have been fattened at the feedlot with hormones, corn meal and the inability to move. The basic diet of our ancestors that will help you control your diabetes is lean and clean protein foods along with complex carbohydrates in their natural state.

WHAT ARE THE "ROOTS" OF DIABETES?

Anthropologists (scientists who study the origins of humans) tell us that humans were originally "hunters and gatherers". The Ice Age covered much of the earth with ice, which dramatically altered food availability. So most of our ancestors, until about 25,000 years ago when the ice began receding to its current position, were meat eaters. Meanwhile, glucose, which only comes from plant food, is the most essential fuel in the human body. The brain, lens of the eye, lungs, and kidneys must have glucose to operate properly. The brain is so dependent on glucose that it does not even need insulin to get glucose into the cells, which is unusual, since nearly all other body cells require insulin and the Glucose Tolerance Factor (GTF) to enable glucose to slip in through the cell membrane.

Back to our ancient ancestors. They consumed very little carbohydrates, and what little they consumed had to be quickly shuttled to the cells for fuel, lest the glucose linger in the bloodstream and cause some damage. People who did not eat much plant food, such as those groups from the colder climates in northern Europe, developed an ability to make glucose from the proteins in our diet (called gluconeogenesis). As you will see in upcoming chapters, glucose is sort of a necessary evil for body cells. If just the right amount of glucose goes straight from the intestinal absorption to the body cells and is burned for fuel, then the person feels great and lives a long and healthy life. If too little glucose is available, then the person feels cranky, depressed, forgetful and listless in the condition called hypoglycemia (low sugar levels in the blood). If an excess of glucose starts accumulating outside of the cell, then "glucotoxicity" begins. Glucotoxicity is a slow but lethal process whereby too much glucose outside of the cells triggers a host of destructive pathways throughout the body.

Once farming began, around 8000 years ago in the Middle East, then our ancestors found the ability to settle down, start cities, and begin the processes of civilization. Then, around 1600 AD, came the refining of wheat in northern Europe. This new technique allowed the wheat miller to strip the outer bran and inner germ from the whole wheat kernel for a fine "Queen's white" flour. Around 1700 AD, trade ships would run the triangle of taking  African slaves to the Caribbean, where the ships would pick up cane sugar, molasses, and rum from the southern plantations and bring these products to Europe. Once refined cane sugar was brought to the masses, the health of millions began to deteriorate rapidly. Enter the dawning of the "diseases of civilization", especially diabetes.

Based upon hundreds of scientific studies, Type 2 diabetes is well recognized as a disease that is a consequence of our modern lifestyle:
♥ obesity
♥ too much refined carbohydrates with too little fiber to slow down the absorption of the sugar
♥ sedentary lifestyle
♥ too little minerals (like chromium, magnesium, and vanadium) in our diet due to the negligence of agribusiness
♥ too much fat and the wrong kind of fat in our diet which leads to changes in cell membranes that no longer recognize the role of insulin.

You will learn more about all of these lifestyle factors later. Basically, the bad news is that diabetes is at epidemic proportions in America and getting worse. The good news is that diabetes is lifestyle induced and lifestyle controlled. How much diabetes will influence your quality and quantity of life will largely depend on you. You will reap a thousand fold benefits when you begin to implement these recommendations in your daily living.

THE SLIPPERY SLOPE TOWARD DIABETES

As in most areas of life, there are many shades of gray in between optimal health and the end stage brittle diabetic at risk for losing a limb. Diabetes usually creeps up on people, not unlike heart disease and cancer, and can take years or decades to mushroom into a serious problem. That is why it is important to change the underlying causes of the disease while it is still in its early stages.

In the beginning, "Fred" or "Sarah" started out as reasonably healthy teenagers. They got married, started a career, and had children. Life gets complicated and hectic. There is less time for exercise, like the tennis and golf they used to play together; and more reasons to sit on the couch and snack while watching TV— "vegging out", as we call our American past time.

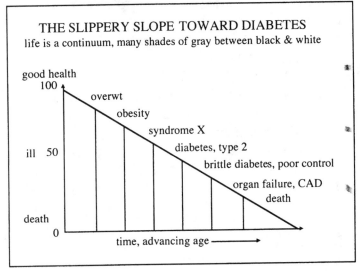

Sarah and Fred start adding a few pounds to the waistline each year. Overweight gradually turns into obesity, which gradually fades into syndrome X (insulin resistance), which eventually turns into diabetes, which can erode into many health problems.

By age 60, both Fred and Sarah are battling a variety of health problems, including kidney failure, heart disease, Fred's erectile dysfunction, Sarah's poor wound healing, and failing vision. Energy and zest for living are a thing of the past.

There are 23 million more Americans like them. As long as you have a pulse, there is hope for reversing diabetes. The sooner you start and the earlier the stage of your disease, the more likely you are to get dramatic results with this program.

"The excessive use of sugar as a food is usually considered one of the causes of diabetes." Encylopaedia Britannica, 1911

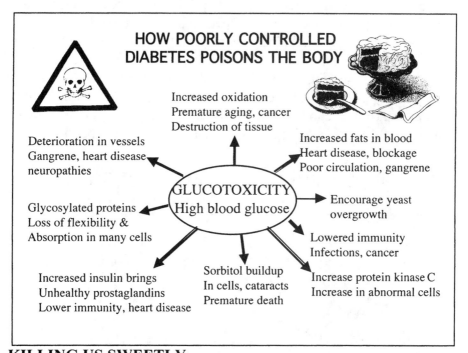

HOW POORLY CONTROLLED DIABETES POISONS THE BODY

Increased oxidation
Premature aging, cancer
Destruction of tissue

Deterioration in vessels
Gangrene, heart disease
neuropathies

Increased fats in blood
Heart disease, blockage
Poor circulation, gangrene

GLUCOTOXICITY
High blood glucose

Encourage yeast
overgrowth

Glycosylated proteins
Loss of flexibility &
Absorption in many cells

Lowered immunity
Infections, cancer

Increased insulin brings
Unhealthy prostaglandins
Lower immunity, heart disease

Sorbitol buildup
In cells, cataracts
Premature death

Increase protein kinase C
Increase in abnormal cells

KILLING US SWEETLY
EXCESS SUGAR AS A WRECKING BALL IN THE BODY

"If you find honey, eat just enough--too much of it, and you will vomit." Proverbs 25:16

Ever marvel at the beauty of a hummingbird in flight? Hummingbirds, sometimes called "flower kissers", flap their wings faster than the eye can see, making their wings look like a blur. Hummingbirds spend all day every day of their short life seeking out sugar. They sip the nectar from flowers and even suck sugar water from your hummingbird feeder if you set one out. No need to worry about killing hummingbirds with too much sugar in their diet, because they are using sugar for its intended purpose: immediate energy for major muscle exertion. Americans are eating and drinking as if they were hummingbirds, in need of an immediate rush of energy from sugar for muscles. But instead we sit at our desks, or in front of the TV, or in a car or airplane seat. It is this great disparity in sugar intake for immediate energy needs, with little muscle movement that generates one of the greatest killers in the history of humanity: glucotoxicity. When excess glucose builds up in the bloodstream, there is an avalanche of dastardly effects that begin to occur.

This chapter is included not to scare you, but to convince you of the urgency in controlling your blood glucose. Over 6 million of the 23 million Americans with diabetes don't know or don't care about the disease. Many diabetics will ignore doctor and nutritionist recommendations because these lifestyle changes seem inconvenient. While high blood sugar does not hurt anyone in the beginning, it

DIFFERENCES in ENERGY METABOLISM BETWEEN NORMAL & DIABETIC CELLS

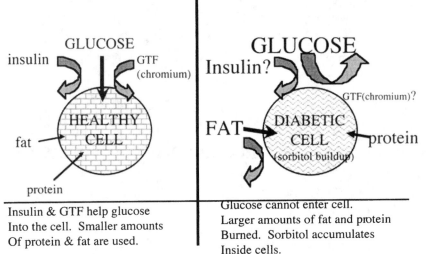

Insulin & GTF help glucose Into the cell. Smaller amounts Of protein & fat are used.	Glucose cannot enter cell. Larger amounts of fat and protein Burned. Sorbitol accumulates Inside cells.

initiates an avalanche of biological problems that cannot be stopped by any drug or nutrient.

While we have known for centuries that poorly controlled diabetes leads to many complications, it was not until recently that scientists could explain how excess glucose poisons the system. Excess blood glucose accumulates outside of the cell. The free glucose begins to attach to various blood proteins in the process of glycosylation...essentially "tanning" these cell membranes (just like tanning cowhide into leather makes it tougher and less flexible) and various proteins to reduce their flexibility and absorption properties.

Meanwhile the cell inside is starving for fuel. So the cell begins to burn fat, but rather inefficiently, leading to higher blood fats circulating through the 60,000 miles of blood vessels. The residue particles of incomplete combustion of fats are called ketone bodies and leave the diabetic with breath like an alcoholic, some confusion, and often a sense of "who cares" about this condition.

Excess sugar in the blood begins a rapid acceleration of the oxidation, or wearing out, of all cells. This oxidation increases the aging process, rusting the nerves to bring neuropathies (or tingling and painful nerves), shriveling the blood vessels in the eyes for possible blindness, starving the kidneys for possible renal failure, and shutting down circulation to the distant extremities for possible gangrene. Excess blood glucose lets a monster out of the bag: protein kinase C, which generates too much cell division, possibly leading to cancer.

It has been well documented that cancer is a "sugar feeder", or an obligate glucose utilizer.[9] There is a direct relationship between countries that eat the most sugar and the incidence of breast cancer. Also, insulin is a powerful growth (anabolic) hormone which can accelerate cancer spread.[10] When the diabetic cannot use or even store the excess blood sugar, opportunistic yeast living in all of us can

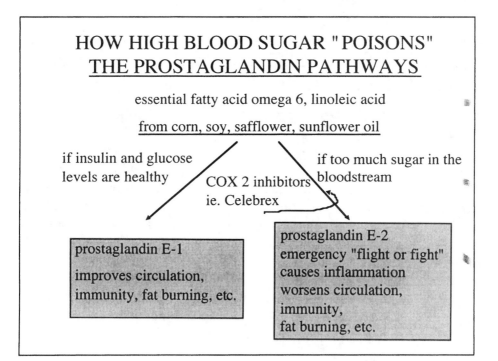

HOW HIGH BLOOD SUGAR "POISONS"
THE PROSTAGLANDIN PATHWAYS

essential fatty acid omega 6, linoleic acid

from corn, soy, safflower, sunflower oil

if insulin and glucose levels are healthy

COX 2 inhibitors ie. Celebrex

if too much sugar in the bloodstream

prostaglandin E-1

improves circulation, immunity, fat burning, etc.

prostaglandin E-2

emergency "flight or fight" causes inflammation worsens circulation, immunity, fat burning, etc.

readily start growing on the sugar and leave the diabetic with a systemic yeast infection, which starts another cascade of health problems.

Excess insulin from insulin resistance, Type 2 diabetes, then starts another cascade of events by switching a "Y" fork in metabolism to make more unfriendly prostaglandin PGE-2, which causes constriction of blood vessels, lowering immunity, increasing the stickiness of all cells (greater risk for heart disease, stroke, and the spreading of cancer), and more. A new category of prescription drugs, called COX-2 inhibitors (stands for Cyclo-OXygenase inhibitors) helps to relieve inflammation caused by too much sugar in the bloodstream forcing the body to make nasty prostaglandins from our excessive intake of omega 6 oils from soy, corn, etc. All these problems stem from something as simple as too much sugar in the blood, or what scientists now call "glucotoxicity".[11]

HOW IS BLOOD GLUCOSE MEASURED?

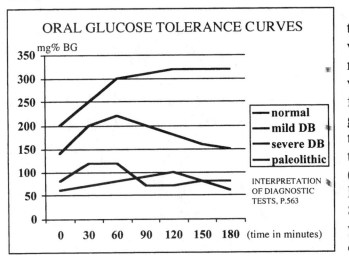

ORAL GLUCOSE TOLERANCE CURVES

mg% BG

legend: normal, mild DB, severe DB, paleolithic

INTERPRETATION OF DIAGNOSTIC TESTS, P.563

(time in minutes)

In order to be diagnosed with diabetes, most clinicians will rely on the fasting plasma glucose (FPG) or the oral glucose tolerance test (OGTT). The FPG requires an 8 hour fast, after which blood is drawn and tested for glucose. The OGTT requires a 12 hour fast after which a blood sample is drawn, then a glass of sweet fluid (glucose solution) is consumed by the patient. Blood samples are drawn every 30-60 minutes for the next 3-6 hours. While the FPG is easier and cheaper to perform, the OGTT provides a more accurate picture of the body's ability to handle blood glucose. Essentially, the diabetic is trying to take the "highs and lows" out of the swings in blood glucose.

EVALUATING BLOOD GLUCOSE LEVELS		
considered to be:	Fasting Plasma Glucose FPG	Oral Glucose Tolerance Test
NORMAL	less than 110 mg/dl	less than 140 mg/dl
PREDIABETES	110-125 mg/dl	140-199 mg/dl
DIABETES	126 or higher	200 or higher

INSULIN RESISTANCE

In 1988, a well respected physician researcher, Dr. Gerald Reaven, of Stanford University Medical Center published his findings on this growing problem of insulin resistance, or Syndrome X.[12] Essentially, a large and growing percentage (25% by Reaven's estimate) of the "healthy" non-obese non-diabetic population in the US are suffering from insulin resistance, which means that the body makes enough insulin, but the insulin cannot seem to "open the door" of the cell membrane to allow glucose to enter the cell. Insulin resistance is a leading cause of Type 2 diabetes, along with rises in hypertension (over 60 million Americans have high blood pressure), and heart disease (still the leading cause of death in the US).

The cell membrane receptor for insulin could be compared to the uniqueness of a fingerprint. This receptor is a 3 dimensional site

THE GATEKEEPER
cell membrane dynamics:

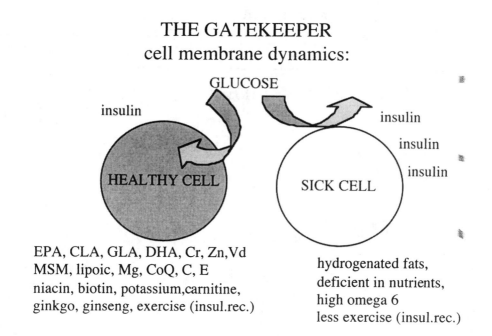

GLUCOSE

insulin

insulin

insulin

insulin

HEALTHY CELL

SICK CELL

EPA, CLA, GLA, DHA, Cr, Zn, Vd
MSM, lipoic, Mg, CoQ, C, E
niacin, biotin, potassium, carnitine,
ginkgo, ginseng, exercise (insul.rec.)

hydrogenated fats,
deficient in nutrients,
high omega 6
less exercise (insul.rec.)

on the cell membrane that must be in proper working order for insulin to do its job. Realize that the average healthy non-diabetic individual secretes around 31 units of insulin daily, while the Type 2 obese diabetic secretes 114 units daily!!! This is nearly 4 times the normal amount. Lean Type 2 diabetics, which are rare, secrete 14 units of insulin daily and Type 1 insulin dependent diabetics make an average of 4 units of insulin each day.[13]

The reason that too much insulin is made and still doesn't do the job is the improper structure from the wrong building materials for the insulin receptors on the cell membrane. This "gatekeeper" of the cell is composed of a fatty (lipid) layer of very specific fats. But Americans feed themselves the wrong kind of fats (hydrogenated, saturated) which become incorporated into the cell membrane and not enough of the right kinds of fats (EPA and DHA from fish, ALA from flax, GLA from borage and primrose, CLA from range fed animals) along with deficiencies of minerals like magnesium, sulfur, chromium, and vanadium that assist in this crucial insulin receptor site on the cell membrane.

DIABETES: A PROBLEM OF HANDLING DIETARY CARBOHYDRATES

Essentially, diabetics have a problem dealing with dietary carbohydrates, which come from bread, potatoes, sweets, and more. So why does the American Diabetes Association tell diabetics to eat more carbohydrates? And why do they not distinguish between fast acting (high glycemic index) and slow acting carbohydrates? This is why the

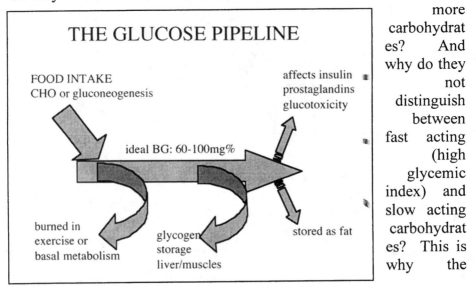

THE GLUCOSE PIPELINE

FOOD INTAKE
CHO or gluconeogenesis

affects insulin
prostaglandins
glucotoxicity

ideal BG: 60-100mg%

burned in exercise or basal metabolism

glycogen storage liver/muscles

stored as fat

incidence of diabetes is climbing and many people with diabetes find little relief in their physician's ADA approved diet.

DOES BLOOD SUGAR IMPACT BREAST CANCER SURVIVAL?

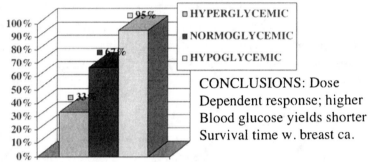

CONCLUSIONS: Dose Dependent response; higher Blood glucose yields shorter Survival time w. breast ca.

STUDY DESIGN: Mice (BALB/C) injected with aggressive mammary tumor and then placed on 3 different diets to alter blood glucose. Survival after 70 days was 8 of 24 (hyper), 16 of 24 (normo) & 19 of 20 (hypo). Santisteban, GA, Biochem.& Biophys Res. Comm., vol.132, no.3, p.1174, Nov.1985

Diana Schwarzbein, MD is a noted physician and board certified endocrinologist who found that offering the high carb diet for diabetics that she was taught in her residency only made the diabetic's symptoms worse. However, when the light switched on in her brain that diabetes is a condition in which people do not handle carbs well, she began offering her patients a "paleolithic diet" which is higher in meat and vegetables and lower in grains and sugars and found major improvements in their ability to control blood glucose.[14]

At age 12 in 1946 Richard Bernstein developed type 1 diabetes. His condition worsened, in spite of being treated by the physician who was then head of the American Diabetes Association. Richard started experimenting with a low carbohydrate diet and found that his symptoms improved dramatically. He tried to convince his doctor of the merits of this diet, to no avail. No one would listen to him. So he went back to medical school while in his 40s and is now a board certified endocrinologist whose diabetes is a minimal inconvenience to his life and helps to instruct patients through his clinical practice and his book on the merits of a low carbohydrate diet for diabetics.[15]

The basics of controlling diabetes is to eat very few quick acting carbs, eat less carbs all together, make the cells more receptive to absorbing insulin and glucose via the right fats and micronutrients, and exercise more to burn off the sugar in the bloodstream. Its all about regulating the "glucose pipeline", which is the constant stream of carbs from the diet into the blood that diabetics do not properly manage. Old joke: Patient walks into a doctor's office and says (while lifting his arm above his head) "Doctor, everytime I do this its hurts." "Then don't do that" says the brilliant doctor. Diabetics have problems metabolizing dietary carbs. Then don't do that.

ACTION PLAN

Once you are under a doctor's care for your diabetes, then please do the following basic steps to get your health moving in the right direction:

♥ DETERMINATION. Have a firm conviction that you can improve your health through lifestyle changes such as diet, exercise, and supplements. <u>You can make a difference</u> in the outcome of your diabetes.

♥ LOSE WEIGHT. Gradually begin a weight loss program. 90% of Type 2 diabetics are overweight. Weight loss usually brings considerable improvements in blood glucose regulation and, for some people, return to a healthy weight brings complete remission of the diabetes.

♥ EAT WHOLESOME NATURAL FOODS. Eat a diet of natural unprocessed foods. Shop the perimeter of the grocery store where you will find fresh fruits and vegetables, chicken, turkey, fish, meat, eggs, and whole grain bread. Venture into the "deep dark interior" of your grocery store only to get sacks of dried beans and brown rice.

♥ RATIO OF MACRONUTRIENTS. Mix your food in ratio of about 25% protein, 25% fat, and 50% complex high fiber carbohydrates. This means that looking at your dinner plate, you need to have about 1/3 of the plate covered with lean and clean protein food, such as chicken, turkey, fish, lean beef, pork, or beans. Another 1/3 of your plate needs to be covered with cooked plant foods, such as beans, vegetables, bread, squash, potatoes. The remaining 1/3 of your plate needs to be uncooked and unprocessed plant foods, such as a tossed salad of fresh colorful vegetables. Include the superfoods of brewer's yeast, flax oil, cinnamon, garlic, vinegar, onions, and fish in your diet often.

♥ Drink at least 8 cups of clean water daily.

♥ Get 30 minutes of exercise daily. Brisk walking is the most realistic, since you can do it without a partner, anywhere, anytime.

♥ Take the following nutritional supplements on a daily basis: 500 mg vitamin C, 500 mg niacin (inositol hexanicotinate), 50 mg B-6, 600 mcg B-12, 400 iu vitamin E (mixed tocopherols), 300 mg magnesium citrate, 300 mg sulfur (methyl sulfonyl methane), 6 mg manganese, 10 mg zinc (picolinate), 2 mg vanadyl sulfate, 400 mcg chromium picolinate, 100 mg lipoic acid, 100 mg L-carnitine, essential fatty acids of 1000 mg EPA and 250 mg GLA, 200 mg gymnema sylvestre, 200 mg bitter melon extract, 100 mg ginseng. See Appendix for where to buy items suggested in this book. For a convenient and economical "all in one" vitamin, mineral, herbal, fatty acid supplement, consider buying ImmunoPower EZ (GettingHealthier.com).

♥ Compliance with this program should bring: better control of blood sugar, more energy, better wound healing, better eyesight and lowered risk for eye complications, enhanced circulation to the feet and hands and reversal of "numbness", lowered fats in the blood to prevent heart disease, lowered risk for kidney damage, improvement in mental and physical energy levels.

PATIENT PROFILE: M.V. had been an award winning chef in a major city restaurant when the overeating pushed her into Type 2 diabetes. She already had the beginnings of blurred vision and tingling in the feet when she passed out one night at work. M.V. loved to cook and eat and was distressed when I suggested a new way of eating. However, once she tried some of these recipes, she found an enjoyment that was not found in her heavy sauces. "Clean and unadulterated" whole food became her motto. Demand for her talents at cooking nutritious and delicious foods brought her a pay raise and fame at a different restaurant with her "low fat, low sugar, high taste" cuisine. Her blood glucose and body weight are both within reason and she no longer has problems with poor circulation in her feet or eyes.

ENDNOTES

[1] . Anderson, RA, Proc Nutr Soc. 2008 Feb;67(1):48-53

[2] . Drum, D., et al., TYPE II DIABETES SOURCEBOOK, p.6, Lowell, Los Angeles, 1998

[3] . Jackson, K., Today's Dietitian, vol.5, no.8, p.23, Aug.2003

[4] . Campbell, PJ, et al., Diabetes, vol.42, p.405, 1993

[5] . O'Dea, K., Diabetes, vol.33, p.596, June 1984

[6] . Schmid, RF, NATIVE NUTRITION, p.89, Healing Arts Press, Rochester, VT, 1994

[7] . Price, WA, NUTRITION AND PHYSICAL DEGENERATION, Keats, New Canaan, 1945

[8] . Eaton, SB, et al., New England Journal of Medicine, vol.312, no.5, p.283, Jan.1985

[9] . Rothkopf, M., Nutrition, vol.6, no.4, p.14S, July/Aug.1990 supplement

[10] . Yam, D., Medical Hypotheses, vol.38, p.111, 1992

[11] . Mooradian, AD, Adv in Care of Old People w.Diabetes, vol.15, no.2, p.255, May 1999

[12] . Reaven, GM, Diabetes, vol.37, p.1595, Dec.1988

[13] . Murray, M., ENCYCLOPEDIA OF NATURAL MEDICINE, p.409, Prima Publ, 1998

[14] . Schwarzbein, D., THE SCHWARZBEIN PRINCIPLE, Health, Deerfield Bch,FL, 1999

[15] . Bernstein, RK, DR. BERNSTEIN'S DIABETES, Little, Brown, & Co., Boston, 1997

CHAPTER 11
CANCER
CAN WHOLE FOODS PREVENT
OR DELAY THE ONSET OF CANCER?

"I have been wrong. The bacteria is nothing. The terrain is everything." Louis Pasteur 1822-1895 co-founder of microbiology

FROM NATURE'S PHARMACY: Apigenin

Researchers at the University of California Irvine discovered a substance only found in fruits and vegetables that helps cells to die when their time has come. Programmed cell death, or apoptosis, is an intense area of research in cancer, because cancer cells "forget" to die. It is this loss of apoptosis that makes cancer such a difficult disease to treat and usually creates chemo resistance, so that even if  the chemo was working in the beginning, it stops working due to this cellular glitch in cancer cells. Apigenin is a substance found in fresh fruits and vegetables that causes p53 to make cancer cells die and even increases the kill rate when cancer cells are given chemo. This study was funded by the National Institutes of Health and published in Proceedings of the National Academy of Sciences.[1] We have known for centuries that a diet rich in fruits and vegetables was protective against cancer and many other diseases. With modern science we are beginning to understand "why" this works.

Cancer is now the number one cause of death in America, surpassing heart disease as of January 2005. Over 4 million Americans are currently being treated for cancer, with another 4 million "in remission", and possibly awaiting a recurrence of the cancer. Each year, over 1.4 million more Americans are newly diagnosed with cancer with another 1 million skin cancers that are treated on an outpatient basis at the doctor's office. Half of all cancer patients in general are alive after five years. 42% of Americans living

CANCER INCIDENCE EXPECTED TO INCREASE
due to aging population?

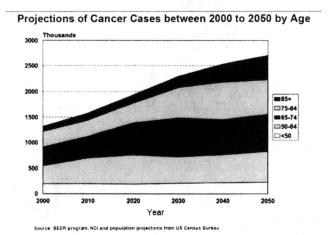

Projections of Cancer Cases between 2000 to 2050 by Age

Source: SEER program, NCI and population projections from US Census Bureau

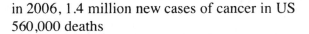

in 2006, 1.4 million new cases of cancer in US
560,000 deaths

today can expect to develop cancer in his or her lifetime. Today, 24% of Americans die from cancer--a sharp contrast to the 3% who died from cancer in the year 1900. Europe has an even higher incidence of cancer. For the past four decades, both the incidence and age-adjusted death rate from cancer in America have been steadily climbing. Some people claim that the recent very modest improvements in cancer survival are explained by earlier diagnosis from more cancer screening procedures such as PSA, colonoscopy, breast exam, etc. Ironically, amidst the high-tech wizardry of modern medicine, at least 40% of cancer patients will die from malnutrition, not the cancer itself.

PREVENTING CANCER WITH WHOLE FOODS

Cancer is not a new phenomenon. Archeologists have discovered tumors on dinosaur skeletons and Egyptian mummies. From 1600 B.C. on, historians find records of attempts to treat cancer. In the naturalist Disney film, "Never Cry Wolf", the biologist sent to the Arctic to observe the behavior of wolves found that the wolves would kill off the easiest prey, which were sometimes animals suffering from leukemia. Cancer is an abnormal and rapidly growing tissue, which, if unchecked, will eventually smother the body's normal processes. Cancer may have been with us from the beginning of time, but the fervor with which it attacks modern civilization is unprecedented. Over 563,000 Americans die annually of cancer, or roughly 1,544 people per day.

President Richard Nixon declared "war on cancer" on December 23, 1971. Nixon confidently proclaimed that we would have a cure for cancer within 5 years, by the 1976 Bicentennial. However, by 1991, a group of 60 noted physicians and scientists gathered a press conference to tell the public "The cancer establishment confuses the public with repeated claims that we are winning the war on cancer... Our ability to treat and cure most cancers has not materially improved."[2] The unsettling bad news is irrefutable:

⇒ newly-diagnosed cancer incidence continues to escalate, from 1.1 million Americans in 1991 to 1.6 million in 1998

⇒ deaths from cancer in 1992 were 547,000, up from 514,000 in 1991

⇒ since 1950, the overall cancer incidence has increased by 44%, with breast cancer and male colon cancer up by 60% and prostate cancer by 100%

⇒ for decades, the 5 year survival has remained constant, for non-localized breast cancer at 18% and lung cancer at 13%

⇒ only 5% of the $1.8-3 billion annual budget for the National Cancer Institute is spent on prevention

⇒ grouped together, the average cancer patient has a 50/50 chance of living another 5 years, which are the same odds he or she had in 1971

⇒ claims for cancer drugs are generally based on tumor response rather than prolongation of life. Many tumors will initially shrink when chemo and radiation are applied, yet tumors often develop drug-resistance and are then unaffected by therapy.

⇒ within the next few years, cancer is expected to eclipse heart disease as the number one cause of death in America. It is already the number one fear.

⇒ 42% of Americans living today can expect to develop cancer

Preventing and reversing cancer. It has now been well accepted that proper nutrition could prevent from 50-90% of all cancer.[3] It has also been well documented that various nutrients can reverse pre-malignant conditions, including: folic acid and cervical dysplasia (abnormal cells in the cervix), vitamin A and oral leukoplakia (mouth lesions), vitamin E and fibrocystic breast disease, folic acid and bronchial metaplasia (abnormal cells lining the lungs). Each of these conditions are "regionalized cancers" that have not yet sprung forth into the rest of the body. The next step is for metastasizing cancer.

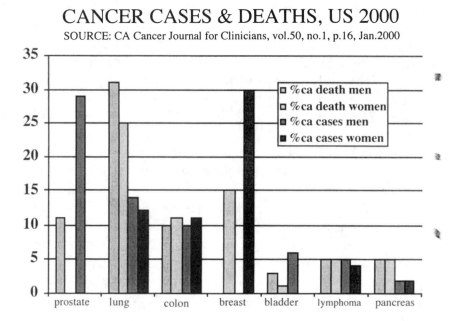

CANCER CASES & DEATHS, US 2000

SOURCE: CA Cancer Journal for Clinicians, vol.50, no.1, p.16, Jan.2000

APOPTOSIS: programmed cell death
healthy cells have it, cancer cells don't
nutrients help to induce apoptosis in cancer cells

National Library of Medicine: number of articles on...
apoptosis: 43,728
apoptosis & vitamin A: 504
apoptosis & vitamin D: 210
apoptosis & vitamin E: 202
apoptosis & vitamin C: 165
apoptosis & selenium: 79
apoptosis & olive oil: 7
apoptosis & tomato (lycopene): 3
apoptosis & fish oil: 62
apoptosis & borage oil (GLA): 11

Since it has become clear that a "magic bullet" against cancer is not expected in our lifetime, the wisest course for all of us is to make significant efforts to prevent cancer through lifestyle, including proper nutrition. Nature provides us with an incredible array of anti-cancer substances in a mixed diet of whole foods:

HISTORICAL PRECEDENCE. The link between nutrition and cancer has long been recognized. Over 2000 years ago, Chinese medical texts referred to "an immoderate diet" increasing the risk for esophageal cancer.[4] Throughout the early 20th century, epidemiological and animal lab data continued to accumulate showing that a diet high in fat and/or low in vitamin A elevated the risk for cancer. By 1964, the evidence was sufficient for the World Health Organization panel, headed by the noted authority Sir Richard Doll, to issue a tidy little pamphlet on the causes of cancer, including nutrition. By 1982, the National Academy of Sciences in America endorsed the nutrition to cancer link with their technical book, DIET, NUTRITION, AND CANCER. The Surgeon General of the United States published a book, NUTRITION AND HEALTH, in 1988 which further detailed the link between nutrition and cancer. By 1990, the Office of Technology Assessment, an advisory branch of Congress, completed its book, UNCONVENTIONAL CANCER TREATMENTS, in which they gave credibility to the use of nutrition in cancer treatment and predicted that nutrition would "rise the ranks into clinical respectability" as adjunctive therapy for cancer patients.[5] The first and second international scientific symposia on "Adjuvant nutrition in cancer treatment" were held in 1992 and 1994, gathering world reknowned experts in medicine and biochemical research to support the notion that "a well-nourished cancer patient can better manage the disease".[6]

YOUR BODY "KNOWS" HOW TO HEAL ITSELF

There is overwhelming scientific evidence supporting the statement "a diet rich in fruits and vegetables lowers the risk for cancer". Professor Block at the University of California Berkeley has counted nearly 200 studies in humans showing that the higher the intake of fruits and vegetables the lower the risk for cancer, with the people consuming the most cutting their cancer risk in half compared to the people consuming the least fruits and vegetables.[7]

A SAMPLING OF CANCER ANTAGONISTS FOUND IN VARIOUS FOODS
(WITH ACTIVE INGREDIENT IN PARENTHESES)[8]:

>inhibitors of covalent DNA binding

broccoli & cabbage (phenethyl isothiocyanate)

fruits, nuts, berries, seeds, and vegetables (ellagic acid)

fruits & vegetables (flavonoids in polyphenolic acid)

>inhibitors of tumor promotion

orange & yellow fruits & vegetables (retinol)

nuts & wheat germ (vitamin E)

fruits & vegetables (vitamin C)

green, orange, & yellow fruits and vegetables (beta-carotene)

garlic & onions (organosulfur compounds, reduce the formation of organosoluble metabolites and increase the formation of water soluble metabolites which are easier to excrete)

curry/tumeric (curcumin)

chili peppers (capsaicin, a vanillyl alkaloid)

>inducing biotransformation

cabbage, brussel sprouts, spinach, cauliflower and broccoli (indole-3-carbinol)

seafood & garlic (selenium)

>reducing the absorption of carcinogens

fruits, vegetables, grains & nuts (fiber)

fruits & vegetables (riboflavin chlorophyllin)

THE PROTECTIVE ACTION OF VITAMINS AGAINST CANCER INCLUDES[9]:

>preventing the formation of carcinogens

>increasing detoxification

>inhibiting transformed cell replication

>controlling expression of malignancy

>controlling differentiation processes

>enhancing cell to cell communication

FRUIT, SUGAR, AND CANCER

In basic biochemistry, sugar is a simple carbohydrate molecule that is soluble in water. Sugars generally end with ..."ose", like glucose, fructose, etc. Theoretically, the fructose from corn syrup should have a similar effect on the body as the fructose from fresh fruits. But that has not been the case. Researchers find convincing evidence that fructose from corn syrup, which is added to many processed foods and soft drinks, has a major role in causing non-alcoholic fatty liver disease.[10] Meanwhile, natural fructose in fresh whole fruit seems to play a protective role against cancer and other diseases. In the study illustrated below, doctors at Harvard found that a higher intake of fruit was associated with a lower risk of prostate cancer. We are only beginning to fully appreciate the elegant symphony of nutrients found in fresh wholesome foods.

DOES FRUIT (SUGAR?) CAUSE CANCER?

whole fruit is rich in phytochemicals, antioxidants (ORAC),
apoptosis agents, enzymes, low glycemic index

risk for prostate ca.

STUDY DESIGN:
Prospective study of 47,781
men 1986-1994; 1369 cases
prostate cancer. "Fruit
intake inversely associated
with risk of advanced
prostate cancer." 47%
lower risk in higher fruit
intake (>5 servings/day)
vs. lower intake <1 serving.

Giovannucci, E., et al., Cancer Res., vol.58, no.3, p.442, Feb.1998

NUTRIENTS CAN REVERSE PRE-MALIGNANT LESIONS

>Vitamin C and beta-carotene are effective at reversing cervical
dysplasia and oral leukoplakia in humans.[11]
>Vitamin A derivatives (retinoids) reverse bronchial metaplasia in
humans.[12]
>Combination of folate and vitamin B-12 reversed bronchial
metaplasia in humans.[13]
>Injections of vitamin E, beta-carotene, canthaxanthin (a carotenoid)
and algae extract dramatically bolstered levels of tumor necrosis factor
alpha and reversed hamster buccal pouch tumors.[14]
>58 adults with familial adenomatous polyps (near 100% progression
to cancer if untreated) were entered into a randomized study providing
high dose vitamin C with E and high fiber, or placebo plus low fiber
diet. The high fiber group experienced a limited degree of polyp
regression.[15]

Can Nutrients Reverse the Cancer Process?

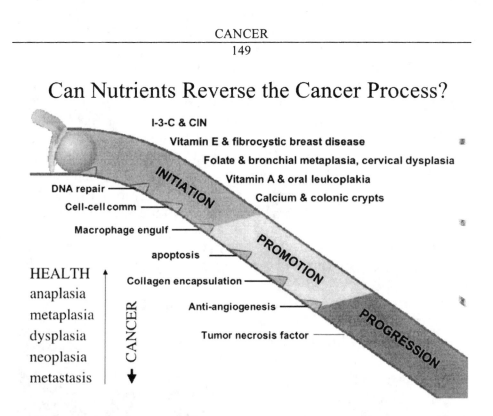

I-3-C & CIN

Vitamin E & fibrocystic breast disease

Folate & bronchial metaplasia, cervical dysplasia

INITIATION

DNA repair

Vitamin A & oral leukoplakia

Cell-cell comm

Calcium & colonic crypts

Macrophage engulf

apoptosis

PROMOTION

HEALTH
anaplasia
metaplasia
dysplasia
neoplasia
metastasis

CANCER

Collagen encapsulation

Anti-angiogenesis

Tumor necrosis factor

PROGRESSION

HOW DO FOODS PROTECT US FROM TOXINS AND CANCER?

-By spurring on the body to produce more toxin scavengers, like glutathione peroxidase from indoles in cabbage.

-By bolstering the immune system. Once the external therapies of chemo, radiation and surgery have eliminated the visible tumor, then the real and final cancer battle is totally dependent on the immune factors. Many foods and individual nutrients are influential here.

-By stimulating certain detoxifying enzyme systems, like the liver's cytochrome P450.[16] Selenium, vitamin C and milk thistle help here.

-By shutting down the oncogene in human cells, that acts like a traitor to participate in cancer growth. Soybeans, vitamin A and D help here.

-By directly killing tumor cells. The bioflavonoid quercetin, vitamin C, B-12, K, and garlic help here.

-By directly killing bacteria or viruses that may cause cancer.

-By binding up substances, like bile acids, that can decay into a carcinogenic substance. Fiber is a champion here.

-By caging carcinogenic heavy metals, in a process called chelation (say 'key-lay-shun'), and carrying these toxic minerals out of the body. Bioflavonoids, vitamin C and garlic help this way.

-By attaching to fats, to stop the carcinogenic fat "rusting" process. Calcium, vitamin E and fiber use this method.

-By providing the known essential and unknown important nutrients that the body needs to better defend itself against pollutants.[17]   A well-nourished body is better able to detoxify, neutralize and excrete the ubiquitous poisons of the 20th century.

IF YOU HAVE BEEN DIAGNOSED WITH CANCER, THEN CONSIDER THE FOLLOWING SUGGESTIONS:

HOPE, OPTIMISM, AND A FIGHTING SPIRIT

Focus on the parts of your body that are working properly, not on the cancer. Since you are alive enough to read this book, then something and perhaps quite a bit are working in your body.   Give thanks for everything that you can think of. Thanksgiving is a healing balm on the body and soul.

Be enthusiastic. The word "enthusiasm" comes from the Greek words meaning "God within". With joy, enthusiasm, appreciation, and altruism, we literally become a conduit for God's life itself.

KNOWLEDGE, OPTIONS, DATA GATHERING

While your doctor who made the cancer diagnosis may have a plan for you, it is probably not the only therapy that is appropriate for your cancer and may not even be the best therapy. You need to explore your options. In today's society, getting information is easier than ever before. Get on the Internet and spend a few hours gathering data and phone numbers on who can help you with your particular cancer. The more knowledge that you have on the treatment and curing of your cancer, the more likely you are to make the right decision on which "wagon master" to choose for your vital treatment ahead.

Consider hyperthermia as primary or adjunctive therapy for your cancer. The following can provide a detailed report on doctors around the world who have a successful track record in treating your cancer:

➤ Janice Guthrie, Health Resource, ph.800-949-0090
➤ Greg Anderson, CancerRecovery.org, ph.800-238-6479
➤ Frank Wiewel, People Against Cancer, ph.515-972-4444
➤ Susan Silberstein, PhD, Cancer Education, ph.610-642-4810
➤ Steven Ross, PhD, World Research Foundation ph.520-284-3300

STARVE THE CANCER

Cancer is a sugar-feeder. The scientists call it an "obligate glucose metabolizer". You can slow cancer growth by lowering the amount of fuel available to the tumor cells. Americans have become humming birds in our constant consumption of sweet fluids and foods. The resulting constant high blood glucose levels yield many diseases, including cancer, diabetes, heart disease, hypertension, and yeast infections. Trying to beat cancer while eating a diet that constantly raises blood glucose is like trying to put out a forest fire while someone nearby is throwing gasoline on the trees.

Stop eating refined sugars, like white sugar and corn syrup. Begin an exercise program to burn blood glucose down to a manageable level. Your cancer is not going to be happy as you begin to starve it. You will develop sugar cravings worse than you currently have. Ignore them and push through the discomfort.

Make fish, fruit and colorful vegetables the staples in your diet. Use cinnamon liberally, since it helps to stabilize blood glucose. Take supplements of chromium and magnesium. I have yet to see a cancer patient beat the disease who continued to load up on the average amounts of sugar in our diet, which is 140 pounds per year per person.

NUTRITION + MEDICINE= IMPROVED RESULTS

While chemotherapy and radiation can kill cancer cells, these therapies are general toxins against your body cells also. A well-nourished cancer patient can protect healthy cells against the toxic effects of chemo and radiation, thus making the cancer cells more vulnerable to the medicine. Proper nutrition can make chemo and radiation more of a selective toxin against the cancer and less damaging to the patient.

THE HEALING POWER OF WHOLE FOODS

It is amazing how simple the answer to cancer can be. Our brilliant researchers have spent 37 years and $70 billion of your tax dollars wrestling with the complex issue of curing cancer. Yet Nature has been solving the dilemma for thousands of years. All of us get cancer all of the time, yet magical ingredients in a whole food diet are there to help the body beat cancer. Ellagic acid from berries induces "suicide" in the cancer cells. Lycopenes from tomatoes help to suppress cancer growth. Genistein in soy, glutathione in green leafy vegetables, and S-allyl cysteine in garlic are examples of the new scientifically-validated cancer fighters of the 21st century.

You don't have to wait for 5 years while some drug company goes through the $700 million drug approval process, nor for FDA approval, nor for a doctor's prescription for some drug that has many toxic side effects and costs thousands of dollars each month. These miracle anti-cancer agents are waiting patiently at your nearby grocery store and health food store.

❖ Eat foods in as close to their natural state as is possible.
❖ Eat as much colorful vegetables as your colon can tolerate.
❖ If a food will not rot or sprout, then throw it out.
❖ Shop the perimeter (outside aisles) of the grocery store.

CHANGE THE UNDERLYING CAUSE

No one with a headache is suffering from a deficiency of aspirin. And no one with cancer has a deficiency of chemo or radiation. While these therapies might temporarily reduce tumor burden, they do not change the underlying cause of the disease.

Mrs. Jones might be suffering from metastatic breast cancer because, in her case, she is still hurting from a hateful divorce of 2 years ago, which drives her catecholamines into a stress mode and depresses her immune system; she goes to bed on a box of high sugar cookies each night; she has a deficiency of fish oil, zinc, and vitamin E; and she has an imbalance of estrogen and progesterone in her body. Her oncologist may remove the breasts, give her Tamoxifen to bind up estrogen, and administer chemo and radiation; but none of these therapies deals with the underlying causes of the disease. And it will come back unless these driving forces for the disease are reversed.

ILLNESS AS A TEACHING TOOL

Many a cancer patient has stood in front of an audience and said: "Cancer is the best thing that ever happened to me." If you are nodding in agreement with this statement, then you are moving toward healing.

3 PATIENT PROFILES: MULTIPLE MYELOMA

M.G.T. was diagnosed with advanced multiple myeloma. His doctors told him that chemo might extend his life to a year and without chemo he would succumb to the disease in much less time. Michael Gearin-Tosh pursued alternative cancer treatment aggressively, using whole food diet, supplements, intravenous vitamin C and detoxification. He went in to complete remission, considered impossible by his first oncologist, and remained disease free for eight years before writing LIVING PROOF: A MEDICAL MUTINY in 2002.

J.H. was a successful attorney and family man when he was diagnosed with multiple myeloma in 2002. He followed my recommendations for aggressive whole food diet and supplement support while undergoing an autologous (using his own stem cells) then allogeneic (using his sister's stem cells) transplant procedure. His doctors were surprised at how well J.H. tolerated the rigors of a double stem cell transplant. James Huston is in good health as of 2005, enjoys his family, continues to fly (he was a former top gun Navy pilot), practice law, and write bestsellers like SECRET JUSTICE.

K.Q. was 39 when he was diagnosed with multiple myeloma. His oncologist told K.Q. to "eat whatever you want" and if K.Q. used any nutrition supplements during chemo that K.Q. would have to find another oncologist. K.Q. was given an assortment of chemo agents, plus decadron steroids, thalidomide and more. K.Q. died in intensive pain and on a ventilator 18 months later while his wife was pregnant with twins. K.Q. was my brother in law, Kevin Quinn. In my opinion, aggressive chemo or radiation therapy without aggressive protective nutrition therapy constitutes malpractice in medicine.

ENDNOTES

[1] . Cai X, et al "Inhibition of Thr55 phosphorylation restores p53 nuclear localization and sensitizes cancer cells to DNA damage" PNAS 2008; DOI: 10.1073/pnas.0804608105.

[2]. Ingram, B., Medical Tribune, vol.33, no.4, p.1, Feb.1992

[3]. Quillin, P, HEALING NUTRIENTS, Random House, NY, 1987

[4]. U.S. Dept. Health Human Services, THE SURGEON GENERAL'S REPORT ON NUTRITION AND HEALTH, p.177, GPO # 017-001-00465-1, Washington, DC, 1988

[5]. Office of Technology Assessment, Congress of United States, UNCONVENTIONAL CANCER TREATMENTS, p.14, OTA-H-405, U.S. Government Printing Office, Washington, DC, September 1990

[6]. Quillin, P, Williams, RM (eds.), ADJUVANT NUTRITION IN CANCER TREATMENT, Cancer Treatment Research Foundation, Arlington Heights, IL, 1994

[7] . Block G, Patterson B and Subar A: Fruit, vegetables, and cancer prevention: A review of the epidemiologic evidence. Nutr Cancer 18:1-29, 1992. see also Block G: Vitamin C and cancer prevention: The epidemiologic evidence. Am J Clin Nutr 53:270S-282S, 1991.

[8]. Byers, T., et al., Patient Care, vol.11, p.34, 1990

[9]. Weisburger, JH, American Journal Clinical Nutrition, vol.53, p.226S, 1991

[10] . Lê KA, Bortolotti M., Curr Opin Clin Nutr Metab Care. 2008 Jul;11(4):477-82., see also Rutledge AC, Adeli K.
, Nutr Rev. 2007 Jun;65(6 Pt 2):S13-23.

[11]. Singh, VN, et al., American Journal Clinical Nutrition, vol.53, p.386S, 1991

[12]. Gouveia, J, et al., Lancet, no.1, p.710, 1982

[13]. Heimburger, DC, et al., Journal American Medical Association, vol.259, p.1525, 1988

[14]. Shklar, G., et al., European Journal Cancer Clinical Oncology, vol.24, no.5, p.839, 1988

[15]. DeCosse, JJ, et al., Journal National Cancer Institute, vol.81, p.1290, 1989

[16]. Boyd, JN, et al., *Food Chemistry and Toxicology*, vol.20, p.47, 1982

[17]. Quillin, P., SAFE EATING, p.129, M.Evans, NY, 1990

APPENDIX
FOODS HIGH IN SPECIAL NUTRIENTS

"Nature, to be commanded, must be obeyed." Francis Bacon

FOODS HIGH IN BETA CAROTENE

(milligrams per 3 1/2 ounces—100 grams)

Apricots, dried	17.6 (about 28 halves)
Peaches, dried	9.2 (about 7 halves)
Sweet potatoes, cooked	8.8 (about 1/2 cup mashed)
Carrots	7.9 (about 1 1/4 medium carrots)
Collard greens	5.4 (about 1/2 cup)
Kale	4.7 (about 2/3 cup, chopped)
Spinach, raw	4.1 (about 1 1/2 cups)
Apricot, raw	3.5 (about 3 medium)
Pumpkin	3.1 (about 1/2 cup mashed or canned)
Cantaloupe	3.0 (about 1/10 melon)
Beet greens	2.2 (about 2/3 cup cooked)
Squash, winter	2.4 (about 1/2 cup mashed)
Romaine lettuce	1.9 (equal of 10 leaves)
Grapefruit, pink	1.3 (about 1/2 grapefruit)
Mango	1.3 (about 1/2 mango)
Green lettuces	1.2 (about 10 leaves)
Broccoli, cooked	0.7 (about 2/3 cup)
Brussels sprouts	0.5 (about 5 sprouts)

FOODS HIGH IN CALCIUM

(milligrams per serving)

Ricotta cheese: 1/2 cup	337
Parmesan cheese: 1 ounce	336
Milk: 1 cup	300
Calcium-fortified orange juice: 1 cup	300
Mackerel with bones: canned: 3 ounces	263
Yogurt, no fat: 4 ounces	225
Salmon with bones, canned: 3 ounces	191
Collards, frozen, cooked: 1/2 cup	179
Dried figs: 5 figs	135
Sardines, with bones: 1 ounce	130
Tofu, firm: 1/2 cup	118
Turnip greens, fresh, cooked: 1/2 cup	99
Kale, cooked: 1/2 cup	90
Broccoli, fresh, cooked: 1/2 cup	89
Okra, frozen, cooked: 1/2 cup	88
Baked beans: 1/2 cup	80
Soybeans, cooked 1/2 cup	65
Chickpeas, cooked: 1/2 cup	60
White beans, cooked: 1/2 cup	45
Pinto beans, cooked: 1/2 cup	40

FOODS HIGH IN FOLIC ACID

(micrograms per serving)

Chicken livers, simmered: 1/2 cup	539
Bulgur, cooked: 2/3 cup	158
Okra, frozen, cooked: 1/2 cup	134
Orange juice, fresh or canned: 1 cup	136
Spinach, fresh, cooked: 1/2 cup	130
White beans, cooked: 1/2 cup	120
Red kidney beans, cooked: 1/2 cup	114
Orange juice, frozen, diluted: 1 cup	109
Soybeans, cooked: 1/2 cup	100
Wheat germ: 1 ounce	100
Asparagus, fresh, cooked: 1/2 cup	88
Turnip greens, fresh, cooked: 1/2 cup	85
Avocado, Florida: 1/2 fruit	81
Brussels sprouts, frozen, cooked: 1/2 cup	79
Lima beans, dry, cooked: 1/2 cup	78
Chickpeas, cooked: 1/2 cup	70
Sunflower seeds: 1 ounce	65
Orange sections: 1 cup	54
Broccoli, fresh, cooked: 1/2 cup	53
Mustard greens, fresh cooked: 1/2 cup	51
Beets, fresh, cooked: 1/2 cup	45
Raspberries, frozen: 1/2 cup	33

FOODS HIGH IN POTASSIUM

(milligrams per serving)

Blackstrap: 1/4 cup	2,400
Potato, baked: 1 medium	844
Cantaloupe: 1/2 fruit	825
Avocado, Florida: 1/2 fruit	742
Beet greens, cooked: 1/2 cup	654
Peaches, dried: 5 halves	645
Prunes, dried: 10 halves	626
Tomato juice: 1 cup	536
Yogurt, low-fat: 1 cup	530
Snapper: 3 1/2 ounces	522
Lima beans, dried, cooked: 1/2 cup	517
Salmon: 3 1/2 ounces	490
Soybeans, cooked: 1/2 cup	486
Swiss chard, cooked; 1/2 cup	483
Apricots, dried: 10 halves	482
Orange juice, fresh: 1 cup	472
Pumpkin seeds: 2 ounces	458
Sweet potato, cooked: 1/2 cup	455
Banana: 1 fruit	451
Acorn squash: 1/2 cup	446
Almonds: 2 ounces	426
Spinach, cooked: 1/2 cup	419

Herring: 3 1/2 ounces	419
Milk, skim: 1 cup	418
Mackerel: 3 1/2 ounces	406
Peanuts: 2 ounces	400

FOODS HIGH IN SELENIUM

(micrograms in 100 grams or 3 1/2 ounces)

Brazil nuts	2,960
Puffed wheat	123
Tuna, light, canned in water	80
canned in oil	76
Tuna, white, canned in water	65
canned in oil	60
Sunflower seeds, roasted	78
Oysters, cooked	72
Chicken liver, cooked	72
Wheat flour, whole grain	71
Clams, canned	49

Note: Organ meats are generally high in selenium, as are whole grains. Most fruits and vegetables are generally low in selenium; the highest is garlic with 14 micrograms per three and a half ounces.

FOODS HIGH IN ZINC

(milligrams per serving)

Oysters, smoked: 3 ounces	103
Oysters, raw, without shell: 3 ounces	63
Crabmeat, steamed: 2 medium	4
Crabmeat, cooked: 1/2 cup	6
Pot roast, braised: 3 ounces	7
Calf's liver, cooked: 3 ounces	7
Turkey, dark meat, roasted: 3 1/2 ounces	5
Pumpkin and squash seeds: 1 ounce	3

Note: Meat and poultry are generally high in zinc. Many cereals have about 4 milligrams of zinc per serving.

FOODS HIGH IN VITAMIN C

(milligrams per serving)

One guava	165
Red sweet pepper: 1 pepper	141
Cantaloupe: 1/2 fruit	113
Pimientos, canned: 4 ounces	107
Sweet green pepper: 1 pepper	95
Papaya: 1/2 fruit	94
Strawberries, raw: 1 cup	84
Brussels sprouts: 6 sprouts	78
Grapefruit juice: from 1 fruit	75
Kiwi fruit: 1 fruit	74
Orange: 1 fruit	70
Tomatoes, cooked: 1 cup	45
Orange juice, in carton	
or from concentrate: 1/2 cup	52
Broccoli: 1/2 cup cooked	49

Tomato juice: 1 cup	45
Grapefruit: 1/2 fruit	42
Broccoli: 1/2 cup raw	41
Cauliflower, raw: 1/2 cup	36
Peas, green, raw: 1/2 cup	31
Kale, cooked: 1/2 cup	27

FOODS HIGH IN VITAMIN D

3 1/2 ounces	International Units (IU)
Eel	4,700
Pilchard	1,500
Sardines, fresh	1,500
Herring, fresh	1,000
Salmon, red	800
Salmon, pink	500
Mackerel	500
Salmon, chinook	300
Herring, canned	225
Salmon, chum	200
Tuna	200
Milk (nonfat, low-fat whole)*	100

*8 fluid ounces.

FOODS HIGH IN VITAMIN E

Vitamin E is fat-soluble and thus is concentrated in vegetable oils, nuts and seeds, legumes and brans. Vitamin E is almost nonexistent in animal foods. Vitamin E is destroyed on exposure to heat.

(milligrams per 3 1/2 ounces)

Nuts and Seeds	
Sunflower seeds	52
Walnuts	22
Almonds	21
Filberts (hazelnuts)	21
Cashews	11
Peanuts, roasted	11
Brazil nuts	7
Pecans	2
Brans and legumes	
Wheat germ	28
Soybeans, dried	20
Rice bran	15
Lima beans, dried	8
Wheat bran	8
Oils	
Wheat germ	250
Soybean	92
Corn	82
Sunflower	63
Safflower	38
Sesame	28
Peanut	24

APPENDIX

GOOD NUTRITION REFERENCES:
Anderson, WELLNESS MEDICINE, Keats, 1987
Balch & Balch, PRESCRIPTION FOR NUTRITIONAL HEALING, Avery, 1993
Eaton, PALEOLITHIC PRESCRIPTION, Harper & Row, 1988
Grabowski, RJ, CURRENT NUTRITIONAL THERAPY, Image Press, 1993
Haas, STAYING HEALTHY WITH NUTRITION, Celestial, 1992
Hausman, THE RIGHT DOSE, Rodale, 1987
Hendler, DOCTOR'S VITAMIN AND MINERAL ENCYCLOPEDIA, Simon & Schuster,1990
Lieberman, S. et al., REAL VITAMIN & MINERAL BOOK, Avery, 1990
Murray, M, et al., ENCYCLOPEDIA OF NATURAL MEDICINE, Prima, 1990
National Research Council, RECOMMENDED DIETARY ALLOWANCES, Nat Academy, 1989
Price, NUTRITION AND PHYSICAL DEGENERATION, Keats, 1989
Quillin, P., HEALING NUTRIENTS, Random House, 1987
Shils, ME, et al., MODERN NUTRITION IN HEALTH & DISEASE, Lea & Febiger, 1994
Werbach, M, NUTRITIONAL INFLUENCES ON ILLNESS, Third Line, 1993

WHERE TO BUY NUTRITION PRODUCTS BY MAIL ORDER

BULK FOODS
BulkFoods.com
WaltonFeed.com
Deer Valley Farm, RD#1, Guilford, NY 13780, ph. 607-764-8556
Jaffe Bros. Inc., 28560 Lilac Rd., Valley Center, CA 92082, ph. 760-749-1133
Timber Crest Farms, 4791 Dry Creek, Healdsburg, CA, 95448, ph. 707-433-8251, FAX -8255

BUYING NUTRITION SUPPLEMENTS ON THE INTERNET
GettingHealthier.com
Lef.org
iHerb.com

VRP.com
VitaCost.com
TidHealth.com
TheHealthGuide.com
ImmunoPower.com
MotherNature.com
TheHealthDepot.com
NatureMade.com

**LARGE STORES THAT
SELL VITAMINS,
MINERALS, & SOME
HERBS BY MAIL**
NutriGuard, 800-433-2402
Life Extension Foundation,
888-741-5433
Health Center Better Living,
800-544-4225
Vitamin Research Products,
800-877-2447
Vitamin Trader, 800-334-9310
Willner Chemists, 800-633-
1106

**STORES THAT
SPECIALIZE
IN SELLING HERBS BY
MAIL**
Gaia Herbals, 800-757-9731
Frontier Herbs 800-786-1388;
fax 319-227-7966
Blessed Herbs 800-489-HERB;
fax 508-882-3755
Trout Lake Farm 509-395-
2025
San Francisco Herb Co. 800-
227-4530
StarWest 800-800-4372

**RECOMMENDED
COOKBOOKS**
Super Seafood, Tom Ney
Eat Well, Live Well, Pamela
Smith
Natural Foods Cookbook, Mary
Estella
The Healthy Gourmet Cookbook,
Barbara Bassett
How to Use Natural Foods
Deliciously, Barbara Bassett
Eat Smart for a Healthy Heart
Cookbook, Dr. Denton Cooley
Simply Light Cooking, Kitchens
of Weight Watchers
Healthy Life-Style Cookbook,
Weight Watchers
The American Health Food Book,
Robert Barnett, Nao Hauser
The Chez Eddy Living Heart
Cookbook, Antonio Gotto Jr.

**DIABETES SUPPORT
ORGANIZATIONS**
American Diabetes Association,
1701 N. Beauregard St.,
Alexandria, VA 22314; ph.800-
342-2383; www.diabetes.org
Canadian Diabetes Association,
15 Toronto St.#800, Toronto,
Ontario M5C 2E3, ph.800-226-
8464, www.diabetes.ca
Central Diabetes Program, US
Indian Health Services, 5300
Homestead Rd NE, Albuquerque,
NM 87110, ph.505-248-4182;
www.ihs.gov